King Hammurabi c

Blackwell Ancient Lives

At a time when much scholarly writing on the ancient world is abstract and analytical, this series presents engaging, accessible accounts of the most influential figures of antiquity. It re-peoples the ancient landscape; and while never losing sight of the vast gulf that separates antiquity from our own world, it seeks to communicate the delight of reading historical narratives to discover "what happened next."

Published

King Hammurabi of Babylon
Marc Van De Mieroop

In Preparation

Cleopatra
Sally Ann-Ashton

Constantine the Great
Timothy Barnes

Pericles
Charles Hamilton

Julius Caesar
W. Jeffrey Tatum

Alexander the Great in His World
Carol Thomas

King Hammurabi
of Babylon
A Biography

Marc Van De Mieroop

Blackwell
Publishing

BLACKWELL PUBLISHING
350 Main Street, Malden, MA 02148-5020, USA
9600 Garsington Road, Oxford OX4 2DQ, UK
550 Swanston Street, Carlton, Victoria 3053, Australia

The right of Marc Van De Mieroop to be identified as the Author of this Work has been asserted in accordance with the UK Copyright, Designs, and Patents Act 1988.

First published 2005 by Blackwell Publishing Ltd

3   2007

Library of Congress Cataloging-in-Publication Data

Van De Mieroop, Marc.
   King Hammurabi of Babylon : a biography / Marc Van De Mieroop.
      p. cm. — (Blackwell ancient lives)
   Includes bibliographical references and index.
   ISBN 978-1-4051-2659-5 (hb. : alk. paper) — ISBN 978-1-4051-2660-1 (pbk. :
alk. paper) 1. Hammurabi, King of Babylonia. 2. Babylonia—History. 3.
Babylonia—Kings and rulers—Biography. I. Title. II. Series.

   DS73.35.V36 2004
   935'.02'092—dc22

                                                        2004013272

A catalogue record for this title is available from the British Library.

Set in 10/13pt Trump Mediaeval
by Graphicraft Ltd, Hong Kong

The publisher's policy is to use permanent paper from mills that operate a sustainable forestry policy, and which has been manufactured from pulp processed using acid-free and elementary chlorine-free practices. Furthermore, the publisher ensures that the text paper and cover board used have met acceptable environmental accreditation standards.

For further information on
Blackwell Publishing, visit our website:
www.blackwellpublishing.com

FSC
Mixed Sources
Product group from well-managed
forests and other controlled sources
Cert no. SGS-COC-2953
www.fsc.org
© 1996 Forest Stewardship Council

Contents

Illustrations

Preface

Hammurabi is one of the few names from Ancient Mesopotamia that is recognized by many people today, although the man lived thirty-eight centuries ago. His renowned law code, carved on a two-and-a-quarter-meter-high stone stela on exhibit in the Louvre Museum in Paris, has guaranteed that fame and defines it. King Hammurabi is celebrated as a lawgiver, whose code is the best known and most eloquent testimony of the legal thoughts of the people of the ancient Middle East. His close to 300 laws prescribe what to do in cases of theft, murder, professional negligence, and many other areas in the daily lives of the people whom he ruled. They are often regarded as the earliest expression of ideas of justice, which are still with us today. Hammurabi deserves to be remembered for the fact that he carved laws on stone, but there are many other aspects to this king's achievements: he was a ruler, warrior, diplomat, and administrator. Those facets are also revealed to us in testimonies of his own time, not on stone stelae but on numerous clay tablets excavated in modern-day Iraq and eastern Syria, and are less known to the general public. They do, however, show a fascinating and multifaceted man, one not always as benign as he wanted to be remembered.

The center of Hammurabi's world was greater Babylonia, the south of today's Iraq from Baghdad to the Persian Gulf. He was in direct contact with more distant regions, from southwestern Iran to north-western Syria. He knew of kingdoms and rulers farther afield. Throughout the whole Middle East, from Iran to the Mediterranean coast and from Anatolia to Egypt, existed scores of small states ruled by local dynasties. Some were more powerful than others; some conquered their neighbors and created larger kingdoms, but those lasted not for very long. Even Egypt, a country that had for centuries been politically unified, was at the time fragmented under competing royal houses. For a short while Hammurabi would change the political layout of his world, since he established through conquest a state that stretched for some 400 kilometers along the Tigris and Euphrates rivers inland from the Persian Gulf. While this creation was ephemeral, it was part of a general evolution throughout the Middle East that would change a system of city-states to one of territorial states.

Hammurabi accomplished all this in the last third of a long reign, which lasted from 1792 to 1750 BC. He was thus not just a man of peace, who provided justice to his people, but also one of war, who initiated fundamental changes in the ancient history of the Middle East with his conquests. We can study these multiple aspects through an extensive documentation from his time that includes his diplomatic correspondence and that of his contemporaries. This material shows him to be a crucial figure in world history, and possibly the earliest one for whom we can write a detailed biography.

In the writing of this book I have benefited much from the assistance of Seth Richardson during his time as a postdoctoral fellow at Columbia University. His appointment was made possible by a generous grant from the Joseph Rosen Foundation. Various colleagues kindly provided some of the illustrations and the permissions to use them: Lamia al-Gailani Weir and Donny George (Iraq Museum), Ulla Kasten (Yale Babylonian Collection), and Jean-Claude Margueron (Mission archéologique de Mari). Stephanie Dalley gave me the permission to reproduce a drawing from her book *Mari and Karana*. I am extremely grateful to all these people and organizations.

Marc Van De Mieroop

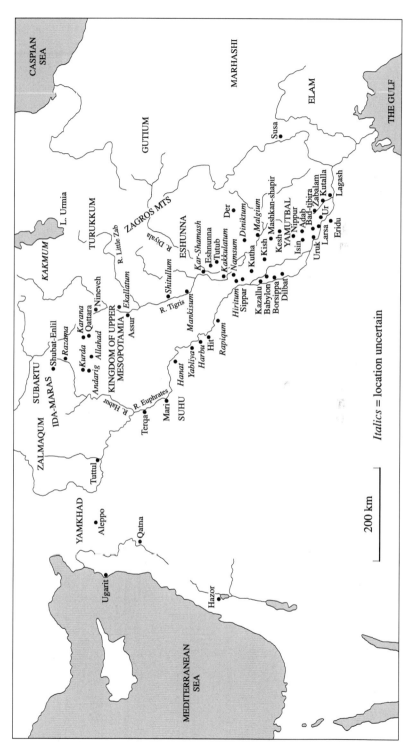

The Middle East in the time of Hammurabi

A Note on Chronology

The dates of the beginning and the end of Hammurabi's reign used in this book are 1792 to 1750 BC. This sounds much more certain than it is in reality. The chronology of early Mesopotamian history and how it relates to the Common Era is not fully clear, and scholars have suggested different systems that place the reign of Hammurabi about 70 years earlier or later. The chronology suggested here is the most commonly found in scholarship, however.

The Babylonian year did not coincide with the modern one, but started some time in March–April. Moreover, it was based on a lunar calendar that is about six days shorter than the length of a year today. Most Babylonian years were 12 months of 30 days each long, but some had 13 months to make up for the difference in length between lunar and solar years. When scholars assign absolute dates BC to a year in the reign of a king (e.g., Hammurabi's first year is 1792 BC), they seem to suggest that the last month of that year was the equivalent to our month December. That is not the case, and most likely would have coincided with March of 1791 BC. In order not to complicate descriptions, I will make use of statements such as "at the end of 1792," with the intent to indicate the end of the Babylonian year.

Abbreviations

Most of the letters quoted in this book are published in two series of volumes that provide editions and translations in French, German, or English. The references will be made to these series.

Letters from Mari are primarily published in the French series *Archives royales de Mari*, abbreviated as ARM.

ARM I = Dossin, G. 1950. *Correspondance de Šamši-Addu et ses fils*. Paris: Imprimerie nationale.

ARM II = Jean, Ch.-F. 1950. *Lettres diverses*. Paris: Imprimerie nationale.

ARM IV = Dossin, G. 1951. *Correspondance de Šamši-Addu et ses fils (suite)*. Paris: Imprimerie nationale.

ARM V = Dossin, G. 1952. *Correspondance de Iasmaḫ-Addu*. Paris: Imprimerie nationale.

ARM VI = Kupper, J. R. 1954. *Correspondance de Baḫdi-Lim*. Paris: Imprimerie nationale.

ARM XIII = Dossin, G. et al. 1964. *Textes divers*. Paris: Librarie orientaliste Paul Geuthner.

ARM XIV = Birot, M. 1974. *Lettres de Yaqqim-Addu gouverneur de Sagarâtum*. Paris: Librarie orientaliste Paul Geuthner.

ARM XXV = Limet, H. 1986. *Textes administratifs relatifs aux métaux*. Paris: Editions Recherche sur les Civilisations.

ARM XXVI/1 = Durand, J.-M. 1988. *Archives épistolaires de Mari I/1*. Paris: Editions Recherche sur les Civilisations.

ARM XXVI/2 = Charpin, D. et al. 1988. *Archives épistolaires de Mari I/2*. Paris: Editions Recherche sur les Civilisations.

ARM XXVII = Birot, M. 1993. *Correspondance des gouverneurs de Qattunân*. Paris: Editions Recherche sur les Civilisations.

Babylonian letters are mostly quoted from the series *Altbabylonische Briefe in Umschrift und Übersetzung*, abbreviated as AbB.

AbB 2 = Frankena, R. 1966. *Briefe aus dem British Museum*. Leiden: E. J. Brill.

AbB 4 = Kraus, F. R. 1968. *Briefe aus dem Archive des Šamaš-ḫāzir*. Leiden: E. J. Brill.

AbB 9 = Stol, M. 1981. *Letters from Yale*. Leiden: E. J. Brill.

AbB 10 = Kraus, F. R. 1985. *Briefe aus kleineren westeuropäischen Sammlungen*. Leiden: E. J. Brill.

AbB 13 = Van Soldt, W. H. 1994. *Letters in the British Museum Part 2*. Leiden: E. J. Brill.

Passages from the code of Hammurabi are cited following the recent edition by Roth in 1997. The abbreviation used for it here is CH.

1

The Early Years

Hammurabi became king of Babylon in 1792 BC. He must have been relatively young at the time as he was to remain on the throne for forty-three years, but whether he was in his teens, twenties, or thirties, we do not know. People had a lower life expectancy then than they do today, yet several men of the period are known to have lived into their seventies, and conceivably Hammurabi was among them. His mother's name is unknown. His father was his predecessor on the throne, one Sin-muballit, who himself had ruled for twenty years. They both belonged to a dynasty of independent kings of the city of Babylon and its surroundings that had started to rule around 1900 and would continue to do so until around 1600. These kings are now referred to as the First Dynasty of Babylon, of which Hammurabi was the most illustrious member.

Politically Babylon up until then had been one of the numerous city-states – small territories governed from an urban center – that covered the area of Mesopotamia. Some had very ancient origins going back to before 3,000 BC, others were more recent, and Babylon itself was only some 400 years old by the time Hammurabi ascended the throne. In the first centuries of the second millennium, city-states were scattered from the Persian Gulf to the mountains of southern Turkey, from the west of modern-day Iran to the Mediterranean coast. Most had their palace, the residence of the king and his staff. All had at least one temple, the house of the patron deity of the city at the center of the state. All had an army, whose size depended on the number of inhabitants and the wealth of the state. Because these states were often close together and needed agricultural fields to feed their populations, conflict was a regular part of their interactions. From our point of view, four millennia later and filtered through the lens of the ancient sources, it may even seem that they were constantly at war with one another. At times, one city was militarily successful enough that it conquered wide territories and ruled supreme for a while – a few decades or a century – but when the central powers waned, the independent dynasties of the subordinate city-states would re-emerge. The city-state ideal was on its way out, however, and a consolidation of territorial control became more common, albeit slowly. Three hundred years before Hammurabi, the city of Ur in the very south of Mesopotamia had united the whole of the region from modern-day Baghdad to the Persian Gulf (the area later called Babylonia), including the city of Babylon. When this union disintegrated, several of the local thrones were seized by men whose background was not in the cities themselves, but among nomadic herdsmen. They spoke a different language from the townspeople, Amorite rather than Akkadian, and had their own cultural traditions and gods. But when they became rulers of the cities, they accepted the ancient urban customs, writing in Akkadian and adopting the practices of the urban rulers in the cult and government. They acknowledged their dual backgrounds, however: they were at once urban kings and tribal sheikhs (the English translations are anachronistic, based on later Middle Eastern terminology, but the distinction is approximately the same).

Hammurabi also had an Amorite ancestry. That was already visible in his name, which, as all names of ancient Mesopotamia, made up a short sentence. Many names used one language only. For example, that of Hammurabi's father, Sin-muballit was fully Akkadian and meant, "The god Sin is the giver of life." The name Hammurabi combined the Amorite word for "family" (*hammu*) with the Akkadian adjective "great" (*rabi*). (Some scholars read it all as Amorite, 'Ammurapi, meaning, "the kinsman heals"). Similarly, his titles also referred to both constituencies: he often employed the common royal title "King of Babylon," referring to his urban role, but sometimes he was "father" or "king of the Amorite land," a tribal affiliation.

Hammurabi's family was far from unique at the time and the mixture of cultural traditions was characteristic throughout the Middle East. In southern Mesopotamia, the ancient Babylonian heritage predominated: a mixture of Sumerian and Akkadian, with Amorite elements. In northern Mesopotamia there were Amorite and Hurrian traditions. In south-west Iran, the local Elamite culture had been strongly influenced by Babylonia, and in western Syria local cultures, Amorite and others, had also accepted Babylonian practices. All over the Middle East the literate culture was Babylonian. The people who wrote, a small minority of the population indeed, did so in that language, using the cuneiform script and the clay tablet developed in southern Mesopotamia in the late fourth millennium. They spoke a variety of languages – Akkadian, Amorite, Elamite, Hurrian, Sumerian, and probably others – but they all wrote in Babylonian when contacting one another.

When Hammurabi succeeded his father, the kingdom of Babylon was some 60 by 160 kilometers in size. His predecessors had expanded it from a small territory around the city of Babylon by integrating some of the neighboring city-states, such as Borsippa, Kish, and Sippar, which remained important cities in the state. They controlled the very northern part of Babylonia, at the spot where the Tigris and Euphrates rivers came the closest together. At Hammurabi's accession, his kingdom was just one among many in the Middle East, and it was hardly the most important. The geopolitical situation was complex and had seen some drastic changes in the preceding decades. Just at the time that Hammurabi became king, King Rim-Sin of Larsa unified the south and center of Babylonia, from the Persian Gulf to the southern border of Babylon. He had accomplished this through the conquest of all his neighbors, culminating in the annexation of Isin, which had dominated central Babylonia since the fall of Ur. Hammurabi thus faced a formidable opponent in the south: Rim-Sin, who must have remembered that Hammurabi's father, Sin-muballit, had joined a coalition with Isin and Uruk against him in 1810, and had skirmishes with him later on.

Hammurabi's neighbor in the north-east was also strong. Across the Tigris along the Diyala river was the state of Eshnunna, whose kings had consolidated power from the Zagros mountains down to the river plain, and had successfully campaigned in areas even further north. They seem to have left Babylon alone, but did assert their rights over the cities that controlled the crossing of the Tigris. For example, several sites now underneath modern Baghdad were firmly held by Eshnunna.

East of the Tigris, some 300 kilometers to the south of Eshnunna, was the powerful state of Elam, whose western capital, Susa, had a venerable history going back to the fourth millennium. Elam was somewhat isolated from the lands between the Tigris and Euphrates as the only route between them ran northward along the foothills of the Zagros and had to pass through the kingdom of Eshnunna. Elam was strong and rich, however, and it seems to have been respected and feared by all. The ruler could intervene in local Babylonian matters, impose his wishes and adjudicate disagreements. In Hammurabi's early years, the ruler of Elam does not seem to have shown any interest in directly annexing parts of the Mesopotamian lands, however, and remained at a distance.

The regional superpower of the time, actively involved in Mesopotamian affairs, was the kingdom of Upper Mesopotamia, far to the north of Babylon. It was the creation of a king called Shamshi-Adad, and his personal history was fully intertwined with that of his kingdom. Shamshi-Adad's origins and early reign are obscure. Like Hammurabi, he was the descendant of Amorites who had seized power in an urban center, but we do not know exactly where they first did so. Shamshi-Adad's father was already an urban ruler, based in an unknown city located possibly between Babylon and Eshnunna, and we know he conducted military campaigns against his neighbors. When Shamshi-Adad succeeded his father, at an unknown date in the late nineteenth century, he took advantage of a temporary weakness of Eshnunna to occupy large parts of northern Mesopotamia. The chronology of events is uncertain, but some details are clear. In 1811, Shamshi-Adad seized Ekallatum, a city on the Tigris. Three years later he captured nearby Assur, one of the oldest cities of northern Mesopotamia, which had a central role in the long-distance trade between Babylonia, Iran, and Anatolia. In 1808, Shamshi-Adad took the throne at Assur and, in order to legitimize his rule, he worked his name and that of his ancestors into the official local king list. Later versions of that document state that he ruled for another thirty-three years.

To the west of the Tigris valley lay the wide and fertile plains of northern Iraq and Syria, as well as the routes to Anatolia and the Mediterranean sea. An expansion in that direction thus had great economic benefits. Although the details are vague, Shamshi-Adad seems to have gradually occupied the existing small kingdoms there, taking some over outright and leaving others under the rule of native kings who became his vassals. His strongest opponent in the west was the kingdom of Mari under Yahdun-Lim, who controlled the Middle Euphrates valley and the southern Habur. The two fought one another over the regions north of Mari and at first Yahdun-Lim was more successful. But his own son, Sumu-Yaman, assassinated him around 1794 and seized the throne of the Mari kingdom. He did not enjoy power for long, however; three years later, in 1796, Shamshi-Adad captured Mari and incorporated its territories into his state.

The kingdom that Shamshi-Adad created, which we call the Kingdom of Upper Mesopotamia, was enormous in size for its time. It stretched over some 400 kilometers from the Tigris to the Euphrates along northern Mesopotamia, and from the border of Babylonia to the Turkish mountains for about the same distance. It was much less densely inhabited than southern Mesopotamia, and much of its territory was too arid for permanent settlements. Despite the already large size of his kingdom, Shamshi-Adad did not rest on his laurels. He continued to campaign in regions beyond, sometimes with his allies, sometimes against them. The extent of his kingdom led him to instate an organizational structure that relied heavily on his sons. Shamshi-Adad set himself up as supreme king in the north of his kingdom, rebuilding an existing city, Shehna, which he renamed Shubat-Enlil. His older son, Ishme-Dagan, who would survive him for a long time and would frequently interact with Hammurabi later on, was made king of Ekallatum to deal with the eastern part of the state. His younger son, Yasmah-Addu, became ruler of Mari and dealt with matters in the west. The father closely supervised his sons, and communicated advice and instructions in letters, many of which were found at Mari. The brothers were also in constant contact with one another, the older often bossing his younger sibling around. Yasmah-Addu was held in low regard by his father. Repeatedly he received admonitions like this:

Don't you have a beard on your chin? When are you going to take charge of your house? Don't you see that your brother is leading vast armies? So, you too, take charge of your palace, your house![1]

Shamshi-Adad was thus not a very supportive father.

The might of the king of Upper Mesopotamia enabled him to impose his wishes on his neighbors, including Hammurabi who ascended the throne some four years after Shamshi-Adad had consolidated his vast state. The two kings had diplomatic contacts and cooperated in certain matters. For example, they came to a power-sharing agreement over the border town of Rapiqum on the Euphrates, with garrisons of both lands living side by side. The cooperation may have been a wise move by Shamshi-Adad to gain allies in his continuous wars. The perpetual search for supporters that would also characterize Hammurabi's later diplomatic adventures was already common in these early days. At one point, Ishme-Dagan reported to his brother Yasmah-Addu:

The ruler of Eshnunna has mobilized all his troops, including palace dependents and free men. Camped at Upi, he multiplies the letters sent to the ruler of Babylon, asking him to join forces and take the city of Mankisum. The Babylonian does not agree.[2]

The city Mankisum controlled the place where the Tigris river could be crossed just to the north of Eshnunna and was at the time in Shamshi-Adad's hands. It would have been an important victory for Eshnunna to capture this strategic place, but the king needed help. Hammurabi wisely kept out of the conflict, however.

Shamshi-Adad was willing to work with Hammurabi, and rendered him small favors. In a letter to Yasmah-Addu he reported that he had tablets copied out for Hammurabi, and that he wanted his son to forward them to the governor of the border region with Babylon, so that they could be delivered. He also repatriated subjects of Babylon that had fled to his country.[3] In return, Shamshi-Adad asked for Hammurabi's help with certain difficulties. One such occasion happened when a mission of delegates from the island of Dilmun, that is modern Bahrain, was under attack and could not reach Mari. Yasmah-Addu wrote to Hammurabi himself and to a friendly official in Babylon to urge them to give shelter to these men. The letter to the official states:

I am sending you Zikriya and Imgurum. They have to guarantee that this mission reaches you in Babylon. I hope that Hammurabi will not be upset by them as they have been there before. I reasoned as follows: "Instead of them coming here and being captured by the enemy, they should go to Babylon and Hammurabi should do what is proper and should give the order that they be protected and that problems be avoided."[4]

Meanwhile, Yasmah-Addu wrote a somewhat less respectful letter to Hammurabi himself:

I am sending you Zikriya and Imgurum. They have to guarantee that this mission reaches you in Babylon. This mission should stay with you until your brother (that is, Ishme-Dagan) writes to you that it should leave.[5]

It seems thus that the ruling family of Upper Mesopotamia saw Hammurabi as a useful ally, but not as an equal.

That things did not always go well for the king of Upper Mesopotamia is clear from other letters. Some cities switched sides from Shamshi-Adad to Eshnunna and it was sometimes hard to punish them. Another letter from Ishme-Dagan to his brother shows that troops could not always be moved fast and that the enemy needed to be deceived to avoid an all-out military response:

When I arrived in Ekallatum, I heard that the city Harbu rebelled and went over to Eshnunna. I have decided to send an army, but there are no boats to carry it across the river at Yabliya. As soon as you receive this tablet send twenty boats with a capacity of one hundred (soldiers) each to Yabliya. If you send empty boats the matter will not remain unnoticed and a spy will warn the enemy. So, ship 1,000 homers of grain, with 100 homers of flour and 10 of beer, at a rate of 50 homers grain per boat, and send them downstream. When you give your orders about these boats, do not mention the numbers of soldiers. When you give orders, give these: "We are sending a convoy with grain rations for the inhabitants of Yabliya, flour and beer mixtures for the citadel of Yabliya."[6]

The last years of Shamshi-Adad seem to have been occupied with continuous campaigning against people from the Zagros mountains, who infiltrated his country from the east, and against his neighbors in the west (Yamkhad) and south (Eshnunna). He portrayed himself as a victorious conqueror, but the reality may have been less illustrious. Probably late in his life he left a relief sculpture depicting himself in battle against a prostrate enemy. On the reverse of the stone he celebrated military victories in the region to the east of the Tigris river:

On the twentieth of the month Addaru, I crossed the Zab river and raided the land of Qabra. I cut down the harvest of that country and I seized all the fortified cities of the land of Arbela in the month Magranum.[7]

Plate 1.1 Victory stela probably commissioned for King Shamshi-Adad. The back of the stela contains an inscription that celebrates military victories in the region east of the Tigris river (Erich Lessing/Art Resource, NY)

The wording of the inscription itself suggests that his actions were nothing more than raids, and we know from another inscription, left by the king of Eshnunna, that Shamshi-Adad had relied on external support in the campaign. When Shamshi-Adad died in 1776 (Hammurabi's seventeenth year) his kingdom disintegrated fast. The people of Mari removed Yasmah-Addu from the throne and Ishme-Dagan could hold on only to Ekallatum and Assur. The fragmentation of power in the Middle East returned for a short while. Soon afterwards an official of the new king of Mari, Zimri-Lim, announced:

No king is truly powerful on his own. Ten to fifteen kings follow Hammurabi of Babylon, Rim-Sin of Larsa, Ibal-pi-El of Eshnunna or Amut-pi-El of Qatna, and twenty kings follow Yarim-Lim of Yamkhad.[8]

The presence of Shamshi-Adad at his northern border probably prevented Hammurabi from being too actively involved in military adventures early in his career. There are some mentions of campaigns in all directions, but the results were certainly temporary. Instead, Hammurabi seems to have focused on the internal development of his kingdom for the first twenty-eight years of his reign. We know of his accomplishments exclusively from Hammurabi's own statements, especially the year-names. These provide only a very partial and biased account, selected tidbits that aimed to portray the king in a positive light. They show that he behaved as a good Babylonian king, providing for his people and his land.

In that role he started off his reign by "establishing justice in the land." This is not a reference to his famous law code, which was issued at the end of his reign, but to a cancellation of outstanding debts, a common royal practice in this period of Babylonian history. The procedure is better known from later examples under Hammurabi's successors, which allow us to reconstruct its elements. Debt was a widespread problem in Babylonian society. People who were financially squeezed because of taxes or special expenses, had to borrow small sums of silver, usually from money-lenders in the cities. Although interest rates were regulated by law to be twenty percent on silver loans and thirty-three and a third percent on those of grain, repayment was difficult, since the full amount was charged even on short-term loans of a few weeks. The people who borrowed were not wealthy, but lived on the verge of financial disaster, and they were easily caught in cycles of increasing debt. They had to pledge their field, house, or even themselves and their children to the creditor, as guarantee for repayment or to provide service as long as the loan was outstanding. Once the creditors had a hold on the debtors' property, they could confiscate the income and charge a fee on the use of the pledged property, so that those in debt were even less likely to repay.

Babylonian kings of the late third and early second millennia intervened in this situation. The ideology of kingship of the time demanded that they free people from such oppression. At irregular intervals they canceled outstanding debts of this nature and released the people in debt-servitude. One of Hammurabi's successors, Ammisaduqa (ruled 1648–1628) left the longest and best preserved declaration of such a royal act. It states in part:

If an obligation has resulted in foreclosure against a citizen . . . and he placed himself, his wife, or children in debt servitude for silver, or as a pledge, he is released because the king has instituted justice in the land; his freedom is in effect.[9]

Edicts of this type aimed to relieve pressure on the common people in society, those who took out loans in times of need. The terms did not affect those who had borrowed in order to finance commercial enterprises. The text of Ammisaduqa's edict clearly stated:

An Akkadian or an Amorite who has received barley, silver, or (other) goods, either as merchandise for a commercial journey, or as a joint enterprise for the production of profit, his document is not voided; he must repay in accordance with the stipulations of his agreements.[10]

In practical terms these cancellations were usually not disastrous for the creditor class. Most of the loans covered were for the payment of taxes and fees to the palace. The creditors who were the intermediaries between the general population and the palace were not forced to pay those either. The edicts resemble a tax amnesty where the palace bore most of the losses. The benefit to the king was that the general population once again became directly responsible to him rather than to private financiers. In ideological terms, the edicts were further important as they showed the king as a guarantor of freedom, confirming his generosity and concern for the people. He annulled the debts at the start of his reign, because this made a new beginning, a clean slate onto which the king would make his mark. If the debt situation got out of hand again later in the reign, new cancellations could be issued at unexpected times, and probably several were inspired by the political convenience of the moment.

Hammurabi thus started off his reign relieving the population of its general debt burden. He is known to have issued at least two later cancellations, one shortly before his thirteenth year when he ruled only Babylon, and one in his thirty-first year. The latter was only in effect in the newly conquered south of Babylonia, and inaugurated his kingship there. With these acts, he was not more or less generous than his fellow rulers would have been, but he simply conformed to the ideals of kingship current at the time.

In other respects he similarly fulfilled his role as a good king. A king took care of the gods. Each city had its patron deity who resided in the temple and was fed and cared for as if a very eminent human being. In smaller towns, the patron deity was only surrounded by a divine spouse and children, each with their own temple or shrine; in larger cities, such as Babylon, numerous gods were honored and many temples existed. The cults could become enormous affairs, with large temples, expensive furnishings and substantial amounts of daily offerings. Private citizens contributed to this, but the king was the major supporter of the gods. Only he could donate objects as expensive as bronze statues or inlaid thrones. Hammurabi did not fail in this respect. In his most eloquent year-name, he claims that he made a throne "finished with gold, silver, semi-precious stones and lapis-lazuli, like a blaze of light for Inanna of Babylon" (year 14). Other year-names and inscriptions left in the temples he built or restored, commemorate numerous other events. Often he focused on cults in Babylon, but other cities in his state, including in newly conquered territories, received his attention as well.

After he took over the southern state of Larsa, for example, he built a temple for the goddess Inanna in the town of Zabalam. The inscriptions left there proclaim:

> After the goddess Inanna gave him a positive omen to govern the land of Sumer and Akkad, and placed its reins in his hands, Hammurabi built the Ezikalama-temple, her cherished house, for his beloved Inanna in Zabalam, the city of which she is the mistress.[11]

In the prologue of his law code, written after his thirty-eighth year, Hammurabi highlighted this aspect of his work. By then he ruled over a wide territory, and in order to declare his control over it, he stated that he had promoted the cults of numerous cities throughout the lands. For example, he proclaimed himself "the one who listens to the god Shamash, the mighty one, who strengthened the foundations of the city of Sippar, who draped the shrine of the goddess Aja with greenery and exalted the temple of Ebabbar which is like a dwelling in heaven."[12] His review of temples passed from one city to another within the kingdom of Babylon, in the conquered territories of Larsa and in regions beyond. A good king took care of the gods and their temples.

But the people under his rule also benefited. As an accomplished king, Hammurabi provided them with plenty. He excavated irrigation canals with such names as "Hammurabi-is-abundance." As fields in lower Mesopotamia could only be cultivated when irrigated, the digging of a canal was an obvious blessing for all. Again, references to such acts by rulers of his time are numerous, and Hammurabi did not fail in this respect. So when late in life he boasted of his accomplishments in the prologue of his law code, he included, for example, that he was "the one who extended the cultivated lands of the city of Dilbat, and who filled the granaries for the powerful god Urash."[13]

A final aspect of his good rule was that he safeguarded his people from danger. He was like a good shepherd who took care of his flock. Those uprooted by war, he settled in peace;

those living in cities, he protected by reinforcing the city walls. In the northern city of Sippar numerous copies of an inscription glorifying such work were preserved. The text includes this statement:

> I raised the top of the foundation of Sippar's city wall with earth so that it was like a high mountain. That mighty wall I built. From the distant past no king among kings had ever made such a wall for my Lord, the god Shamash. I named that wall "At-the-command-of-the-god-Shamash, may-Hammurabi-have-no-rival."[14]

Protection of the people and the land was, of course, also guaranteed by the army, under the king as a great warrior. It is this activity that would fully occupy Hammurabi for four years, from his twenty-ninth to his thirty-second year of rule. In that time he would fundamentally change the political configuration of the Middle East.

2

The Defeat of Elam

To the east of Babylonia, across the Tigris river and the large marshes along its course, lay the ancient land of Elam. It included a wide territory stretching from the Tigris to the highlands of modern-day Fars, some 700 kilometers to the south-east. Elam's western part, governed from the ancient city of Susa, was a lowland watered by several rivers, an environment similar to Babylonia; its eastern part, governed from the city of Anshan, was in the highlands of the Zagros mountains with high mountain peaks and narrow valleys. This duality influenced the political structure of the country in a way that is not fully clear to us. There was a supreme ruler of the entire state of Elam, who bore the ancient title of *sukkalmah*, borrowed from Babylonia. Very prominent next to him was the man in charge of Susa, the western half of the state, who bore the lesser title *sukkal*. The latter had a great deal of independence, including in international affairs where he could represent the entire country. In the days of Hammurabi, a man named Siwe-palar-huppak[1] was the supreme ruler of Elam; the *sukkal* of Susa was Kudu-zulush. Both played an active role in Babylonian affairs.

Because of its dominance in the mountains and its location between Babylonia and the regions further east, Elam was the source of some highly desired materials which were absent in Mesopotamia itself. It controlled one of the few trade routes used to import tin, crucial for the manufacture of bronze tools and weapons, and lapis lazuli, a dark-blue stone that was highly prized for the production of jewelry. Both were mined in the mountains further east in Iran and Afghanistan. Other materials such as hard stone and wood were also brought from Elam into Babylonia for the building of temples and palaces, the manufacture of statues and so on. Elam was, if anything, a wealthier state than the Babylonian principalities.

From its earliest days, some 1,200 years before the reign of Hammurabi, Elam had been in close contact with Babylonia, without really having been part of the system of states in that area. At times contacts were very intense, often at the initiative of Babylonian states. In the twenty-first century, for example, the kingdom of Ur had conquered Elam and ruled it through governors. Because of its size and wealth Elam was able to field impressive armies and regularly it chose to mount invasions of the Mesopotamian lowlands, precipitating political changes there. For example, its campaign around the year 2000 terminated the Ur dynasty that had ruled Elam some decades earlier. The state seems to have preferred to keep its distance from Mesopotamia, however. Sometimes it gave support to Mesopotamian rulers, but it did not attempt to occupy territory. In 1781, for example, it had sent troops to Shamshi-Adad to help him in his campaign against mountain people living in the Zagros, but Elam withdrew immediately afterwards. While Elam did not hold Mesopotamian territory, the kings there seem to have acknowledged the *sukkalmah* as a very important ruler whose authority superseded their own. When they quarreled, they hoped for the latter's support to enforce their claims.

This situation was suddenly changed in 1767, when Elam decided to conquer and occupy certain Mesopotamian states, a policy of overextension that would ultimately lead to its defeat by Hammurabi only two years later. With the death of Shamshi-Adad in 1776 and the fragmentation of his kingdom of Upper Mesopotamia, Eshnunna, located in the Diyala region, had become the strongest power in Mesopotamia. Elam's ruler, Siwe-palar-huppak, knew it blocked his access to the west, and early in 1767 he initiated diplomatic contacts with his colleague in Mari, Zimri-Lim. The rulers exchanged ambassadors who also brought gifts for the kings. Gold, silver, and wine from Mari were reciprocated with tin, which Zimri-Lim needed for his own bronze manufacture, and could also use in secondary diplomatic trade with states as far west as Hazor in Palestine and Ugarit on the north Syrian coast. The alliance between Mari and Elam was a natural: Elam saw Eshnunna as a barrier to its contacts with Mesopotamia, while Mari wanted to thwart the king of Eshnunna, Ibal-pi-El II, who had made military incursions into its territory and supported a rebellion of tribesmen against the Mari palace. An account of presents sent out from Mari on the eighth day of the second month of 1767 shows that Babylon was already involved as well. It reads:

(several broken lines) to Sheplarpak, the king of Anshan. A silver vase weighing half a pound as present to Kudu-zulush, the king of Susa. A silver vase weighing half a pound issued to Ishkur-mansum, the ambassador of Babylon.[2]

Late in 1766 or early in 1765, this coalition turned against Eshnunna under Elam's leadership. The details are vague, but we know the results: the king of Eshnunna, Ibal-pi-El II, disappeared from the scene and his capital was raided. Some of the other cities in his territory seem to have been destroyed[3] and direct rule from Susa was imposed on the region. Contrary to its earlier practice, Elam was here to stay. Officials claiming to be servants to Kudu-zulush were active in the region, and Kudu-zulush himself at times resided in Eshnunna.

It is clear that Siwe-palar-huppak did not see Hammurabi and Zimri-Lim as equal partners, but as subordinates. Nor did he want them to be too close to one another. Thus, he issued commands as a supreme ruler. He demanded from Hammurabi that he return cities he had conquered in Eshnunna's territory to Elam:

The cities of Eshnunna that you hold, do they not belong to me? Release them and submit them to my yoke, otherwise I will pillage your country! My army would set out to the city Mankisum, and it would cross the river at that spot. At the head of my army I myself would cross the river and invade your country.[4]

At the same time he ordered Zimri-Lim via his ambassador to cut contacts with Babylon:

Tell your master that his messengers should no longer go to Babylon and that Babylonians should no longer go to your master.[5]

His intentions to extend his control over Mesopotamia through military means are shown when he demanded troops from Hammurabi for a planned invasion of Larsa:

I have decided to start a campaign against Larsa. Mobilize your elite troops, your siege engineers and the subjects that I saw in Eshnunna, so that they will be ready at my arrival. If one man whom I saw before is not ready, I will hold you responsible.[6]

Hammurabi played along and answered:

As you have written to me, my army is ready and available for your attack. The moment you attack, my army will leave to assist you.[7]

But the king of Elam was playing a dangerous diplomatic game. At the same moment, he sent similar messages to Rim-Sin of Larsa asking him for his support against Babylon. When the two Mesopotamian rulers compared notes, they saw Elam's duplicity and agreed to join forces. Yarim-Addu, the representative of Zimri-Lim in Babylon, reported to his master:

The tablet that the *sukkal* of Elam had sent to Rim-Sin, Rim-Sin sent on to Hammurabi, and Hammurabi likewise sent the tablet that the *sukkal* of Elam had sent him to Rim-Sin. From that moment on, Hammurabi gave orders to his minister of foreign affairs, Sin-bel-aplim, and to one of the administrative secretaries, and he has sent them to the kingdom of Larsa. They are residing with Sin-muballit at Mashkan-shapir, while a minister of Rim-Sin resides with Hammurabi. News from Rim-Sin regularly reaches Hammurabi, and news from Hammurabi regularly reaches Rim-Sin.[8]

Mari seems nevertheless to have remained loyal to Elam. The same writer continued:

Messengers of the *sukkal* of Elam regularly come to Hammurabi. They stay one day and the second day he sends them back. The next time that they arrive I will go to them at the palace gate and talk to them. I will ask about the health of the *sukkal* of Elam and I will tell them: "Because my Lord has given a complete report to the *sukkal* of Elam, his father, and he has spoken frankly with the *sukkal* of Elam, his father, I am being detained here for a long time. My Lord has written to Hammurabi, but he has refused to let me go. But now that you are here, I am no longer worried." That is what I will say to them. My Lord should know.[9]

These good relations between Mari and Elam were soon to deteriorate, however, due to Elam's ambitions in northern Mesopotamia, where Zimri-Lim had gradually extended his influence over the years.

The Elamite ruler sent out several armies to invade northern Mesopotamia, using troops from Elam and Eshnunna, and mercenaries from the Zagros mountains. These were commanded by local men from the north, including rulers of small kingdoms there. The *sukkal* relied thus on northern kings who were willing to switch allegiance to him, and provided them with military support. Early in 1765, for example, a man called Kunnam captured the former north Syrian capital of Shamshi-Adad, Shubat-Enlil, and installed himself there as representative of the *sukkalmah* of Elam. More important to Elam, however, seems to have been one Atamrum, a petty ruler of the region who was eager to further his career by offering his services to the great powers.[10] He was first made viceroy of Eshnunna and represented the *sukkal*'s interest in northern Mesopotamia. He then started a siege of the city of Razama, considered of greater importance than Shubat-Enlil at this time. Its ruler Sharriya remained faithful to Zimri-Lim, however, and put up a good fight. A long letter written by a Mari general to his king includes a report of the siege by men who had escaped Atamrum's army:

From the moment that the army arrived at Razama, the people of the city made a sortie and killed 700 Elamite soldiers and 600 soldiers from Eshnunna. After being cut off for ten days, the city elders came out and said to Atamrum: "We are for peace. If your soldiers move the camp to a distance of five kilometers, we will pay you silver." He answered them as follows: "You must be imagining this, 'Let's make a false proposal so that he will clear out his camp and we will have ended Ida-Maras's (i.e., the area of Razama) problems.' If you are really for peace, why did Sharriya not come out himself? Beat it and fortify your city!" The people of the city answered him thus: "This city belongs to Zimri-Lim and our regular army is with him. Don't try to do anything until the master of this city returns."

Sharriya took his precautions, and set up defenses. Moreover, he continued to make sorties and to kill soldiers from Eshnunna. But Atamrum was in the process of building an attack ramp that was closing in on the city. When the front of the ramp had reached the point where the outer wall meets the glacis, the inhabitants reinforced the wall to the left and the right of the ramp as the attackers were breaching the wall. When it was still night the inhabitants climbed through the breach at the ramp, made a sortie and killed half the attackers. They took their bronze lances and shields and hid them in the city. The inhabitants of the city were only thinking of my Master.

Then Atamrum thought up this ploy. He gave bronze spears to thirty vagabonds and tried to intimidate the city by saying: "Why don't you stop thinking about Zimri-Lim. Don't you see that his soldiers are among the attackers?" They answered: "Those are vagabonds that you armed. In five days you will see the real army with Zimri-Lim at its head."

The rumor that my Lord will arrive has reached the (Elamite) army. During the first watch it went on full alert twice. They also said: "Night and day water has to be brought in to the troops from a distance of ten kilometers. Who from a small army of 2,000 to 3,000

men can escape the killing of water carriers when the inhabitants of
the city make sorties and kill many soldiers?" These soldiers are
alert in their camp and are very afraid of my Lord. May my Lord
hurry to save the city![11]

Zimri-Lim sent an ultimatum to Atamrum: "Razama is my
city. Leave the city!"[12] Atamrum turned for help to the *sukkal*
of Elam who was residing in Eshnunna at the time. He asked
for more troops, and, more importantly, begged the *sukkal* to
attack Zimri-Lim directly, thus making it impossible for him
to come to Razama's aid. But the *sukkal* refused. Atamrum
despaired and started to plot against Elam.

It was the events in the south that determined Elam's fate,
however. The *sukkal* of Elam coveted Babylon and sought
support in northern Mesopotamia for an attack on that city. His
messengers visited the local courts, saying: "Stop your squabbles
and come to me. I want to lay siege to Babylon!"[13] Hammurabi
reacted decisively and brought together an enormous coalition to counter Elam. First he sought the help of Zimri-Lim of
Mari. By the middle of 1765, the two kings negotiated a treaty,
of which Hammurabi's part is still preserved:

By (the god) Shamash of heaven, Lord of the land, and (the god) Adad
of heaven, Lord of the decisions, Hammurabi, son of Sin-muballit,
king of Babylon has sworn. From this day on, for as long as I live, I
will be at war with Siwe-palar-huppak. I will not receive servants or
messengers from him, and I will not send those to him. I will not
make peace with Siwe-palar-huppak without the approval of Zimri-
Lim, king of Mari and of the tribal lands. If I consider making peace
with Siwe-palar-huppak, I will confer with Zimri-Lim, king of Mari
and of the tribal lands, to hear if I should not make peace. We will
only make peace with Siwe-palar-huppak jointly. It is with honesty
and sincerity that I swear this oath to my gods, Shamash and Adad,
before Zimri-Lim, son of Yahdun-Lim, king of Mari and of the tribal
lands.[14]

Because the two rulers could not meet in person, they swore
to the treaty in special rituals before witnesses. A letter written

to Zimri-Lim relates that Hammurabi was suspicious and wanted to know that the king of Mari had already done his part. Zimri-Lim's servant reported:

> I stood up before him (Hammurabi) and with Nabum-malik as my witness I said: "My Lord (Zimri-Lim) did not make an alliance with the man of Elam. While sprinkling flour he raised his hand to Shamash and swore: 'I swear that I will not make peace with the man of Elam.' That is what my Lord has sworn, so for what reason can you not swear at the same time?"[15]

Hammurabi's suspicion was quite justified. Up to a few months earlier, Zimri-Lim had kept on sending gifts to the rulers of Elam in order to maintain diplomatic contacts with them. Hammurabi had sent the Nabum-malik mentioned in this report to Mari in order to establish Zimri-Lim's sincerity. The latter could thus testify that the oath Zimri-Lim's representative swore was trustworthy.

Once the king of Mari was on Hammurabi's side, he became very actively involved in levying troops and recruiting allies. This enthusiasm can be well understood, if we remember that Elam's allies were still threatening Mari's territory in northern Mesopotamia. But Elam was a formidable enemy with massive armies at its disposal. Zimri-Lim needed to raise troops both from the nomads and the villagers in his kingdom, not all of whom were eager to fight. The nomads resisted conscription, as was reported to the king:

> It is now five days after the appointed time that I am waiting for the tribesmen, and the troops have still not gathered. Some of them have come out of the steppe, but they are staying in the villages. I have thus twice sent messages to various villages to get them to raise the levy, but they are still not assembled.
>
> If they still do not assemble three days from now, with my Lord's permission, I will kill a criminal who is in prison, cut his head off and parade it from village to village as far as Hudnum and Appan, so that the people become afraid and assemble soon. Then I could take care of the business that my Lord has assigned me fast.[16]

This plan seems to have worked miracles, as the tribes did eventually contribute troops. They were even eager and happy to go to war, a full turn around, if we can believe another report:

The tribesmen that make up the rear guard have arrived. The front and the rear guards are doing well. There are no illnesses or other problems, and not a single man has been lost. Those who belong to the expeditionary forces are also doing well. My Lord should not worry.

Something else: During every expedition I need to listen carefully, as there are always many complaints. Now, during this expedition I am also listening carefully, but there are no complaints. There is nothing but laughs and songs. They are as happy as if they were at home. All they want to do is fight and defeat the enemy. The hearts of my Lord's servants are speaking. My Lord should rejoice![17]

So, in the end, Zimri-Lim sent a large army to Hammurabi. The first contingent consisted of 600 men, followed by 1,300 villagers under the generals Zimri-Addu and Ibal-pi-El. Another reinforcement of unknown size was led by Sharrum-andulli, and, finally, the various tribes of the Mari kingdom contributed contingents. These did not all arrive in Babylon at the same time, but in separate groups. Whenever a new division arrived, it was a big occasion, and a letter from Ibal-pi-El to Zimri-Lim gives great detail about the ceremonies held when a group of tribesmen joined Hammurabi's troops:

When we were on the way, the news of the arrival of tribesmen reached me, and I announced it to Hammurabi as follows: "The tribesmen have arrived. Will my Lord go out to meet them?" That is what I asked him and he answered: "On the fifth (or sixth) of this month, when we are in Babylon, I will decide." That is what he told me.

We did arrive in Babylon and went to the palace gate. After Hammurabi let me in right away, he said: "Come! Let the troops enter the city and take up quarters in the requisitioned houses. Tomorrow morning they will eat in my presence," and then he left.

Then I said to his minister, Sin-bel-aplim: "Every time they enter Mari my Lord comes out for his servants and the standard bearers parade in front of him." I told him that and he answered: "All the tribesmen will eat with my Lord tomorrow. Let the standard bearers parade then." That is what he answered me. Tab-eli-matim and Sin-bel-aplim left with me, and we let the troops enter the city.

The next day I assembled fifty elite soldiers and made them come in to parade. All the tribesmen have taken their meal in the park in the presence of Hammurabi and it was in that park that the standard bearers paraded. Hammurabi was truly happy that the tribesmen arrived, and he handed out presents.[18]

The letter continues with a long inventory of the gifts Hammurabi made to individual high-ranking officers, and to groups of lower ranking officers, soldiers, and standard bearers. The Mari troops did represent a great asset to Babylon and Hammurabi was willing to pay well for their services. While the official rhetoric calls the goods he gave them presents, they were more likely payments, which were actually pocketed by Zimri-Lim, their king. As a result these gifts were accounted for in the Mari archives, as assets to the palace. The administrative record of gifts to the particular contingent mentioned in the letter above is preserved. It reads:

> One *hullum*-ring of 10 shekels, one golden ring with a
>   stated value of 10 shekels,
> their actual (combined) weight is 18 shekels,
> one garment and one shirt: for Bahdi-Addu.
> One round disk of 5 shekels, one golden ring of 5 shekels,
> their actual (combined) weight is 8 shekels,
> one garment and one shirt: for Bihirum.
> One round disk of 5 shekels, one golden ring of 5 shekels,
> their actual (combined) weight is 8 shekels,
> one garment and one shirt: for Sulum.
> For the 10 section leaders: one *hullum*-ring and one silver
>   ring with a stated value of 10 shekels,
> their actual (combined) weight is 18 shekels, a garment
>   and a shirt each.
> For the 22 lieutenants, who include the scribe and the herald:
> one silver ring with a stated value of 10 shekels, one
>   medallion with a stated value of 1 shekel
> the actual value is 7 shekels for the ring and 2/3 shekels for
>   the medallion, a garment and a shirt (each).

For the 50 standard bearers: one silver ring with a stated
value of 5 shekels,
one medallion with a stated value of 1 shekel, the actual
value is 4 shekels for the ring and 2/3 shekels for the
medallion, and a shirt each.
For the 804 soldiers: for each 10 men a medallion with
a stated value of 3 shekels,
or an actual value of 2.5 shekels. Gifts to the soldiers.[19]

Hammurabi thus handed out financial rewards before the men
had started to fight, and tried to make them feel welcome by
eating a meal with them.

Because of the coalition with Mari, Hammurabi could also
rely on the support from the distant, yet very important, king
of Yamkhad, Zimri-Lim's father-in-law. The Mari king also
contacted rulers of the region of Zalmaqum, in northern Syria,
east of the Euphrates river. He informed Hammurabi:

I have dictated a letter to the kings of Zalmaqum, and have sent it to
them by mounted messengers. An answer to it should arrive here,
and from the moment these tributary kings' troops arrive, I will send
them to you.[20]

These troops were eventually sent as well, but their loyalty
was to Zimri-Lim rather than to Hammurabi. A Mari representative stationed in the north reported to his king:

From Zalmaqum came to me Bali-Erah, Samuh-El and Ibal-pi-El on
account of my Lord. I asked them for news and they said: "The
princes of Zalmaqum are saying: 'We owe nothing to Babylon. We
did not give troops to Babylon. It is to Zimri-Lim that we have given
troops.' None of their troops will go to Babylon."[21]

The new soldiers did, however, reinforce Mari's northern
borders, relieving its regular forces to march to the south.
Ishme-Dagan, the son of Shamshi-Adad and king of the
northern country of Ekallatum, also assisted Hammurabi with
an unknown number of men.

The battle lines were drawn. The ruler of Elam relied on forces from his own country, from Eshnunna and the Zagros mountains, and he recalled some troops previously assigned to occupy northern Mesopotamia. Kunnam left Shubat-Enlil, leaving only a small garrison behind under his lieutenant Simti-hullurish. Hammurabi could rely on troops from Mari and Ekallatum, and the support of the distant states of Yamkhad and Zalmaqum in north-western Syria. Several states were uncommitted, including Larsa, the strongest power to the south of Babylon.

The initiative was taken by the *sukkal* of Elam. His army started to lay siege to the city of Upi, located in Babylon's territory just across the border with Eshnunna. The attack pushed Hammurabi into a general mobilization of the men of his state, including merchants, usually exempt from military duties, and he even freed slaves so that they could fight. He also sent messengers to Rim-Sin of Larsa to ask for help, and arrested the remaining envoys of Elam in Babylon.[22] Initially the Babylonian garrison in Upi held out waiting for reinforcements. But these came too late. A letter to Zimri-Lim reads:

The army of Hammurabi that held Upi boarded ships and fled. Enemy troops have entered Upi from the (surrounding) forts. The army of Elam returned to Eshnunna.[23]

The first encounter was thus a loss for Hammurabi, yet Elam's ruler did not push further than Upi and withdrew the bulk of his army to Eshnunna. Early in the next year, 1764, he returned. The Elamite army advanced on the city Mankisum, which controlled an important crossing of the Tigris river. The Babylonians, assisted by troops from Mari, reacted immediately and set up base at the border town of Namsum. At first it was unclear where the Elamites would go next. A Mari general reports:

After the enemy crossed the river opposite from Mankisum, he set up camp and rested. Where will he go? I have not yet found out. That is why I did not write to my Lord.[24]

The Elamites decided to lay siege to the city Hiritum at the northern border of Hammurabi's state, close to the important city of Sippar. At least 30,000 men were involved, an enormous number. The Elamites tried the usual tactic of building assault ramps so that siege engines could be placed against the wall, but the inhabitants of Hiritum prevented this by opening the irrigation canals around the city. The earth of the ramps was washed away. The Babylonians sent an army to relieve Hiritum, including the Mari general Zimri-Addu who regularly reported to his king. A major concern was the elimination of enemy equipment. Thus Zimri-Addu wrote:

On the day that I have sent this tablet to my Lord, my Lord's troops and those of Babylon which are confronting the enemy with its towers and ramps, have attacked and removed the ramps.[25]

At the same time, the Babylonians sent off patrols from Namsum, outflanking the Elamites to raid into Eshnunna's territory itself. The raiders set fire to the fields there and stole cattle, making the Elamites worried about their home base. These forays were not always successful, however; once Zimri-Addu communicated:

I have already written to my Lord that 2,000 of my Lord's men and 3,000 Babylonians left on an expedition under Ibal-pi-El. But as a spy escaped, the enemy could take precautions and these troops came back empty-handed. They camped out near the city of Sha-bassi. Ishar-Lim and other servants of Hammurabi asked them: "How is it possible that 5,000 men came back empty-handed?" That is what Hammurabi's servants wrote to Ibal-pi-El and what Ibal-pi-El wrote to me. Afterwards he took supplies for his troops for ten days. Thus I wrote to him: "As you just told me not to come with you, I tell you this: 'If the omens are good, leave Sha-bassi.' I am sending you lambs so that you can consult the omens and, if they are good, continue the campaign with your troops." This is what I wrote to him.[26]

We can see here some of the competition among the Mari generals, lobbying for their king's favor. Zimri-Addu wanted to make his colleague Ibal-pi-El look bad, and gave thus a long description of his failure to accomplish anything, even though he had 5,000 men under his command.

Elam at this point withdrew: although Babylonian pressure was a factor, the main reason for its retreat was internal dissent in its army. Several generals of Eshnunna were unwilling to fight for the ruler of Elam, and even wrote Hammurabi offering their services:

To our Lord, the king of Babylon say, thus speak your servants. The man of Elam took hold of us using massive force and now he wants to devour your country. You have stood up to him, and there is nothing he can do.[27]

Meanwhile, Atamrum, the northern Mesopotamian king who had unsuccessfully attacked Razama on the *sukkal*'s behalf, abandoned his former master and submitted to Zimri-Lim. He probably exercised *realpolitik*, as that king had amassed an army of 20,000 troops against him. This loss of northern Mesopotamia was too much for the Elamites. They first withdrew to the city Kakkulatum on the Tigris river, which they sacked in an act of scorched-earth policy. Then they moved north to the city Mankisum, with the intent to attack the northern state of Ekallatum. Zimri-Addu again reported to Zimri-Lim:

Today they have brought an informer to me and he said: "The enemy is marching north in the direction of Mankisum with the mass of his army." Moreover, I hear everywhere: "He intends to march on Ekallatum." That is what the informer told me. Whatever I hear, I write to my Lord.[28]

Perhaps because they realized that they were exposed in the back to disloyal troops of Eshnunna, the Elamites stopped at Mankisum. Instead they turned east towards Eshnunna and plundered it. All soldiers there rebelled now, and deserted Elam's army. As their last native king had disappeared, they chose one of their own to become the new ruler, a commoner called Silli-Sin. They expelled all Elamite forces, and the *sukkal*

withdrew to his own territory, pitching camp in the city of Diniktum.

The king of Elam realized he had lost, and sued for peace with Hammurabi. A letter to Zimri-Lim written after the fact reports:

The ruler of Elam had set his sights on the entire country, but then he changed his mind and wanted to devour the land of Babylon. If my Lord's god had not intervened, he would have caused a situation as if the people of Babylon would never have existed. Now, however, when a messenger of the *sukkal* of Elam mentions Hammurabi, he says sweetly: "There is peace."[29]

Hammurabi at first responded positively. Another letter to Mari states:

When the Elamites left Eshnunna and the *sukkal* arrived in Diniktum, Hammurabi sent this message to him: "Why did you not listen to what I told you?: 'The people of Eshnunna will not fail to live up to their reputation as rebels. On the other hand, here you will find loyalty.' This is what I told you." He wrote that to Elam and together with the Babylonian messenger that went to the *sukkal*, Elamite messengers returned to Hammurabi. Hammurabi sent a messenger to my Lord as well. He also allowed the Elamite envoys that had been held in his country for a long time to leave, and their property was given back.[30]

Good relations did not ensue, however. Elam promised support to the new enemies of Hammurabi, Rim-Sin of Larsa and Silli-Sin of Eshnunna, which did not endear him to the Babylonian. Late in 1763, a general wrote this final story to his master Zimri-Lim:

A convoy from Malgium arrived and I asked for news. They told me: "The *sukkal* of Elam is dead." When they told the news to Hammurabi, he was very happy.[31]

Unfortunately for Hammurabi the rumor was untrue, and Elam's ruler was only very ill. Nevertheless, although the *sukkal* of Elam continued to have some effect in international affairs, he ceased by this point to be of major concern.

Hammurabi had been lucky in his fight against Elam, his first major war. He proclaimed proudly that in the year 1764 "with the help of the great gods Hammurabi had defeated the armies of Elam, from as far as Marhashi, of Subartu, Gutium, Eshnunna, and Malgium, which had arisen against him as a great mass, and he established the foundations of Sumer and Akkad." He thus claimed that he had fought against the combined armies of all the regions east of the Tigris. Indeed, men from those districts had confronted him, but far from the full might of these territories had attacked. Hammurabi's actions had been a response to Elamite aggression, not his own initiative. He had used his diplomatic skills to enlist the help of Zimri-Lim of Mari, but had failed to recruit Rim-Sin of Larsa. He was very fortunate that the Elamite ruler had to confront rebellions in his own territory and was ejected from Eshnunna. Consequently the *sukkal* had to withdraw all the way to Elam and henceforth remained only marginally interested in Babylonian affairs. This gave Hammurabi a free hand to pursue further plans in the region.

3

The Annexation of Larsa

During the war with Elam, Rim-Sin of Larsa had kept to the sidelines, ignoring requests for help from Hammurabi. It is not a surprise that Hammurabi had turned to him for support. Although Rim-Sin was an old man by this time, certainly in his late sixties, he governed the largest state by far in southern Mesopotamia. He represented a formidable power and was Hammurabi's greatest competitor in Babylonia proper. Hammurabi did not appreciate the fact that Rim-Sin had refused to join forces with him, and did not forgive him. Once the king of Babylon had defeated Elam, he almost immediately invaded the south, and conquered the region by the end of 1763. This feat was the first major expansion of the Babylonian state.

The kingdom of Larsa had a very prominent and ancient history, going back to around 2000 BC. For two centuries it had shared power in the region of Babylonia with other local states. But, by 1794, it had managed to establish hegemony over the entire region from the Persian Gulf to the border with Babylon through its conquest of the central Babylonian state of Isin. The unification had been accomplished by Rim-Sin, a king who at that moment had already ruled for almost thirty years, succeeding his brother Warad-Sin in 1822. Both were sons of Kudur-Mabuk, a man with an Elamite name, who in 1834 had captured the throne of Larsa and placed Warad-Sin on it. Kudur-Mabuk himself resided in Mashkan-shapir, a city on the north-eastern edge of the state, and his country was known as Yamutbal. He created a political structure similar to that of the kingdom of Upper Mesopotamia under Shamshi-Adad: the father resided in one capital, Mashkan-shapir, while the son became king in an old political center, Larsa. Although Warad-Sin, and later Rim-Sin, were kings at home, they had to listen to their father who could interfere in local affairs.

At Rim-Sin's accession in 1822, his state covered only the very south of Babylonia near the Persian Gulf, stretching northward on the eastern side along the Tigris river. Rim-Sin substantially expanded that state in his first thirty years of rule, fighting against rulers of Uruk, Isin, and even Babylon. These early battles had not been conclusive, however. Rim-Sin's year-name for 1810 commemorates a defeat of the three enemies, while Hammurabi's father, Sin-muballit, states that he defeated Larsa in 1800. Most likely these were exaggerated claims of success, and for a long time there was no true domin-ant power, with some territories and cities changing hands repeatedly. In 1804, Rim-Sin started a series of campaigns that were more successful, however, and over time he occupied all the regions to the north of Larsa. This work was crowned in 1794 when he defeated his main rival, Damiq-ilishu of Isin. The event was considered so important that from that moment on every year-name of Rim-Sin was named after it: the first year after the sack of Isin (= 1793) , the second, the third, and so on (= 1792, etc.), for a period of thirty-one years. In international terms the most important repercussion of the annexation of Isin was that Larsa and Babylon now shared a long border. They were the two remaining powers in southern Mesopotamia, while in the north Shamshi-Adad ruled supreme. This was the political set-up when Hammurabi became king in 1792.

In Hammurabi's early career, previously discussed, some military activity is documented, including against the south. In 1786, he reports a conquest of Isin and Uruk, the latter city only some twenty kilometers north of Larsa. This did not lead to an annexation of the territory, however: we have to see these claims as a continuation of the raids and squabbles that had characterized the region for centuries by then. The attitude changed when Hammurabi responded to Elam's expansionist policy, which set him on an eventual collision course with Larsa. The *sukkal* of Elam made the mistake of contacting both Rim-Sin and Hammurabi independently, asking each one for support in an attack on the other. When they discovered this, Rim-Sin and Hammurabi started to discuss an alliance between themselves. While Hammurabi was defending Upi against Elam, he repeatedly requested support from Rim-Sin. The latter hesitated a long time, and gave only vague promises. At one point he wrote to Hammurabi:

My troops are assembled in my country. May your troops be assembled in your country as well. If the enemy attacks you, my troops and ships will come to your help. Likewise, if the enemy attacks me, may your troops and ships come to my help.[1]

But this was only talk, as the man who reported this letter to Zimri-Lim of Mari remarks: "This is what Rim-Sin wrote to Hammurabi, but their armies have not yet joined forces."[2] The result was that Hammurabi defeated Elam in 1764 without Rim-Sin's support.

With Elam out of the way, Hammurabi was free to attack Larsa. The uneasy balance of power in the region, with a number of equal states, including Babylon, Mari, and Larsa, under the indirect supremacy of Elam, was disturbed. No distant force existed any more to keep the competitors in line, and these could now let their ambitions run wild without fear of retaliation from Elam. According to the Mari representative in Babylon, it was Rim-Sin who started the hostilities, but as Mari was an ally of Babylon this may just have been an excuse. The deterioration of relations was reported to Zimri-Lim as follows:

Concerning Rim-Sin, the king of Larsa, as my Lord has already heard, he has not changed his earlier attitude at all. He is hostile to Hammurabi. Military squadrons of his continuously enter into Hammurabi's country to pillage and steal. Every time they make an incursion, they take something back. The representatives of Rim-Sin have been arrested and are held in the palace. Hammurabi continues to complain about this to me. (broken passage) Now no more messengers of Rim-Sin come to Babylon, and there are no more messengers of Hammurabi in Mashkan-shapir.[3]

As a result, sometime in 1763 Hammurabi declared war on Rim-Sin, justifying it as a pre-emptive act authorized by the gods. A long report found at Mari describes Hammurabi's declaration and his call to arms to his troops:

(broken passage. Hammurabi speaks:) "Those are the evil words Rim-Sin has spoken. No one is with me, beside the great gods who came to my rescue and Zimri-Lim, the king of the Sim'alite tribes, who granted me life more than once. The man from Larsa has pillaged my country. After the great gods have removed the grasp of the Elamite, I did many good things for the man of Larsa, but he did not reciprocate. Now, I have complained to (the gods) Shamash and Marduk, and they have responded with a 'yes.' I did not attack without the approval of the god."

Then Hammurabi spoke to his troops: "Go! May the god march in front of you. If the city opens its gates when you arrive, accept its surrender. Even if the city disdains the oath of Shamash and Marduk, do not harm it. If the city does not open its gates, . . . (broken passage)[4]

Hammurabi was supported in his attack by troops from Mari, which were still under the same commanders who had led them against Elam, Zimri-Addu, and Ibal-pi-El. It is thus possible that the army had never even disbanded and that the attack on the south immediately followed Elam's defeat. The country of Yamutbal was in chaos: Rim-Sin remained in the south in Larsa, while he left the defense of the northern part to his brother Sin-muballit, who sought refuge in the city Mashkan-shapir. The report to Zimri-Lim continues:

Rim-Sin is not with the assembled army, and his soldiers are worried. They express their worries as follows: "Where will the enemy engage us?" Sin-muballit, the brother of Rim-Sin, three generals and (broken word) thousand troops are surrounded in the city Mashkanshapir. The entire country is afraid of the attack and is ready to rebel. Three or four days from now, Mashkan-shapir will have fallen. It will not put up resistance.[5]

The city did indeed soon fall and the road to Larsa lay open to Hammurabi. He received additional support troops from Mari and Malgium, took over the cities Nippur and Isin by the middle of 1763 and quickly reached Larsa. The king of Mari received this report:

My Lord's army fares well. When my Lord's troops reached Hammurabi he was very happy. As he had just conquered Mashkanshapir, the entire country of Yamutbal cried out to Hammurabi: "Long live our Lord!" The army of Yamutbal has made peace with that of Hammurabi. Hammurabi took the head of his armies and laid siege to Larsa. In the last month of the year he started the siege.[6]

Although he was an old man by now, Rim-Sin did not give up easily. Hammurabi built assault ramps and brought in siege engines, and continued to secure additional forces from his allies. Even Atamrum, the old ally of Elam who had switched sides to Zimri-Lim, came to Larsa. Hammurabi received an embassy from Ishme-Dagan of Ekallatum and also contacted his old enemy, the ruler of Elam for help. Meanwhile Rim-Sin tried to obtain support from the king of Qatna in distant western Syria, but the messengers were arrested and imprisoned in Babylon. The number of soldiers involved was enormous: one bulletin sent to Mari mentions 40,000 men on the side of Larsa. How many Hammurabi commanded is unknown, but they included soldiers from Babylon, 2,000 men from Mari, 1,000 from Malgium, plus the "liberated" troops from Yamutbal.

The siege lasted six months, and the inhabitants of Larsa ran out of food (although the truth of that fact is disputed in the letter quoted below). A report to Zimri-Lim says:

All the refugees that fall into our hands tell us: "There is no more grain in the city," while there is grain but they do not know about it. As a substitute for grain they eat(?) straw and the chaff that remains.[7]

Finally, Larsa was taken. The report continues:

After the reinforcements arrived, the Babylonian troops could enter Larsa and take over the walls. This morning the men entered. But Rim-Sin escaped alive.[8]

So, Rim-Sin was able to escape, but not for long. Another letter announces that he was captured and sent to Babylon together with members of his entourage. Hammurabi tore down the city walls of Larsa, but did not raze the city.

There was still great confusion in the land. Tribesmen had taken advantage of the conflict to raid the countryside and Hammurabi used the army to restore order. Zimri-Addu of Mari was still involved, and he informed his king as follows:

About fifty Sutean tribesmen left the city Udanum and marched for thirty kilometers to Larsa. After they raided the district occupied by the Babylonians, they took prisoner one or two men, stole grain and brought it back to Udanum. Hammurabi was told and he asked me to provide 100 armed men. I recruited 100 men from the Khanean and Suhu tribesmen, and put Kibsi-Addu at their head. 200 Babylonians joined them. Thirty Suteans attacked this group, but my Lord's soldiers killed six of them and captured three of them alive, while the Babylonians captured one alive. To our soldiers who brought back prisoners, Hammurabi gave a silver ring of two shekels and a shirt each. To Kibsi-Addu who led them, he gave a lambskin coat and a silver ring of eight shekels. To 650 of my Lord's troops Hammurabi gave two shekels silver for every ten men.[9]

Order was soon restored, and records from the year 1762 indicate that life was back to normal.

Hammurabi did not portray himself as a foreign conqueror in the Larsa region, but as the legitimate successor of Rim-Sin. Here he dated records with the year-name "the year that Hammurabi became king," as if he were a brand new king,

Plate 3.1 Terracotta plaque excavated at Larsa. The image shows the goddess Ishtar who leaps over a city wall and beats a fallen man with her weapon. The plaque may have been made after Hammurabi's conquest of the city to celebrate the occasion (courtesy Iraq Museum)

while at home in Babylon it was acknowledged that he had already ruled for thirty years. When he visited the area, he used Rim-Sin's palace as his own. He behaved as a good ruler should and inscriptions document that he constructed temples in several southern cities (Larsa, Ur, and Zabalam). From that moment on, records in the south are dated with year-names of the Babylonian king. Hammurabi instated his own officials in Larsa to administer the southern territories.

In order to initiate his new rule in the region of Larsa, Hammurabi decreed a cancellation of all outstanding personal debts there, though not in Babylon where he had done the same in his first full year of rule. As was described before, people who had needed to borrow silver or grain from private money-lenders were forgiven those debts. These were usually incurred in order to pay duties and rents to the palace, so the king was ultimately the one who bore the brunt of the financial burden. But the private creditors were affected as well, and some of the Larsa entrepreneurs whose careers we know about went out of business. Hammurabi clearly wanted to start out with a clean slate in Larsa. Was he popular with the local people? Perhaps not: the *sukkal* of Elam wrote, soon after the region's conquest, to the king of Eshnunna, "If the king of Babylon attacks you, fight him and I will invade Larsa. The people of Larsa keep on writing to me."[10] Whether this was empty rhetoric or truth, we may never know.

The conquest and annexation of Larsa was a major military and political feat, and Hammurabi named his thirty-first regnal year after the event: "The year that Hammurabi, the king, with the help of the gods An and Enlil went before the army and, by the supreme power which the great gods had given him, conquered the land Yamutbal and its king, Rim-Sin." For the next two decades southern and northern Babylonia were united as one entity, a situation which would have a lasting impact on the political structure of that area. Although the south would regain independence under Hammurabi's successor, Samsuiluna, there was not a return to the Balkanization that had characterized Babylonia for more than a millennium. Since around the year 3000, the region had been home to a set of cities as political centers, each surrounded by a small territory. The dominant political entities were thus the city-states. There were times when one city-state dominated the others, but these moments of unification were temporary and soon replaced by a return to a system of competing city-dynasties.

That ended with Hammurabi's unification, which was short-lived but seems to have effected a fundamental change. Babylonia never became a region of city-states again, but metamorphosed into a large territorial state with a single capital city whose rulers had varying degrees of control over the countryside. No competing city-states were ever to emerge again. That was the most lasting consequence of Hammurabi's rule in political terms.

Hammurabi's military aggression had paid off: he was now king of the largest state in the region. He was not to rest, however, and turned his attention to further conquests. The large coalition of forces under him had fought for almost two years and the foreign participants were eager to return home. Zimri-Lim of Mari needed his troops to deal with military threats in the north of his kingdom, and wrote to his general Ibal-pi-El who was in Babylon: "Put polite pressure on Hammurabi so that he releases the army before the winter." Ibal-pi-El replied that he did, saying to Hammurabi: "Now that god has removed the enemy and the cold days are approaching, why do you keep onto the servants of your brother? Give me orders to leave, so that the men of the army can return home before the cold." But Hammurabi answered: "I want to see what Eshnunna's intentions are in the next five to ten days. Be quiet. Be quiet!"[11] It was indeed to Eshnunna that Hammurabi was to turn next, an adventure in which he would lose Mari's support.

4

The Overthrow of Eshnunna

Hammurabi had accomplished the conquest of Larsa with an enormous army made up of men from Babylon and Mari. The drain on the military capacities of these states left their northern neighbors poorly supervised, and inspired the kings of the north to seek independence or try to tip the balance of power in their favor without interference of the mighty rulers. Mari's interests in particular were under threat, and Zimri-Lim saw his control over northern Mesopotamia slip. Already during the siege of Larsa, he had tried to get part of his army to return to him, but even after the siege was successful, Hammurabi insisted that they stay to help him pacify the area. Finally, Mari's troops came home to intervene in the highly complicated affairs of the north, which would ultimately involve Babylon as well. Numerous battles occurred between armies of ever shifting alliances in this northern theater, and diplomatic activity was equally intense, to such an extent that we have a very difficult time finding out what exactly happened. Often it seems that two enemies suddenly joined forces or broke apart, and the lack of transitional information can make these actions look contradictory. This was a very volatile period: states changed their stances rapidly and repeatedly. Not all the actors involved were equally important or can be studied to the same extent, and many of these events did not directly affect Babylon. But there were some major players, and Hammurabi was forced to deal with them in order to carry on his expansionist policies. One of the main rivals in the north was the state of Eshnunna, which had already played a role under Elam's rule, but as a now-independent state presented a new obstacle to Hammurabi. This state was the next victim on his list of conquests. Its recent history explains why the conflict between Babylon and Eshnunna was almost unavoidable.

By the beginning of Hammurabi's reign, the kingdom of Eshnunna was centered along the Diyala river from its confluence with the Tigris to the foothills of the Zagros mountains. During the first centuries of the second millennium, kings of the capital city, Eshnunna, had conquered numerous surrounding city-states. The kingdom was strategically located. Four major routes ran through it: one from Babylonia to central Iran along the Diyala river; one that gave Elam access to Mesopotamia; one that connected the Tigris and Euphrates valleys at the point they were nearest one another; and one along the Tigris that linked Babylonia to northern Mesopotamia. Eshnunna was thus an appealing target for anyone who sought to dominate the entirety of Mesopotamia. Conversely, when its own rulers were militarily strong they played a crucial role in the affairs of many states. Culturally, Eshnunna shared many elements with Babylonia, including language and the cuneiform script, architectural and artistic styles, and royal titulary (albeit with local peculiarities). The main deity of the state was the warrior god Tishpak, who was not very popular in Babylonia, but was the patron deity of the dynasty in Eshnunna.

By 1800, Eshnunna was a major player on the Mesopotamian scene and its armies campaigned throughout the north and along the Euphrates river. Shamshi-Adad of the great kingdom of Upper Mesopotamia may even have been its vassal for a while. Years later, when Shamshi-Adad's son Ishme-Dagan sought to ally himself with Hammurabi, the envoy of Zimri-Lim in Babylon compared this action to the father's attitude toward the king of Eshnunna:

Plate 4.1   Statue of an unknown ruler of Eshnunna excavated at
Susa. The inscription on the statue was mostly erased but indicates
that it came from Eshnunna. The man portrayed must have ruled
the city before Hammurabi's conquest, but his exact identity
remains unknown (Erich Lessing/Art Resource, NY)

In all his messages to Hammurabi, Ishme-Dagan writes to him as a
servant. That is exactly what his father did. At first all his father's
letters addressed the prince of Eshnunna as a servant does. Then,
when he had taken control over the entire land because of Eshnunna's
troubles, he called him "brother."[1]

The relations between the kings of Eshnunna and of the kingdom of Upper Mesopotamia were stormy: at times they fought

one another, at other times they joined forces in attacks on others and divided the loot. Early in Shamshi-Adad's career, he had to flee to Babylon to escape from the king of Eshnunna, but late in his life he and another ruler of Eshnunna campaigned together in the Zagros mountains against the local population. This pattern of shifting alliances was typical for the period.

The power vacuum left at Shamshi-Adad's death in 1776 encouraged the then-king of Eshnunna, Ibal-pi-El II, to seek expansion of his own influence. He laid claim to parts of the Euphrates valley and sought to force Zimri-Lim to conclude an alliance with him. He sent a very long letter to the king of Mari, then only in his first year of rule, to explain why he should subject himself to Eshnunna. The tone he used was that of a supreme ruler, a father who advised his son.

To Zimri-Lim say, thus speaks your father Ibal-pi-El. You have sent a messenger to me who told me what you had to say: "May my father send 3,000 men to me, whom I will outfit, so that I can seize the cities that I am besieging and take them from the hostile forces." This is what you wrote. As soon as I heard the message of your servant, I agreed and sent troops under one general, and now those troops are with you.[2]

But this help came at a price. Ibal-pi-El continued to explain that he was supporting Zimri-Lim by attacking Shamshi-Adad's son, Ishme-Dagan, but that he wanted Zimri-Lim to accept his sovereignty over part of the Euphrates valley south of Mari. He then urged submission:

I sent to you a great throne, the sign of kingship. Sit on that throne. The kings around you will see it and know that Eshnunna is your great ally. Just as your father Yahdun-Lim held the hem of (i.e., submitted to) the house of the god Tishpak and that he became strong and expanded his kingdom, you too, to the extent that you become my son, will not cease to look for me and to take hold of my hem. I will give you full satisfaction, I will expand your borders, I will restore the city of Mari to its former glory and make its foundations strong.[3]

He then warned that a contingent of troops from Babylon was on its way to assist Ishme-Dagan against Mari and that these should be stopped. "You should send out an army to confront the Babylonian troops firmly. When Hammurabi hears that my army is to confront him, he will no longer send help."[4]

The last threat may have been effective, as we do not know if Hammurabi's troops helped Ishme-Dagan against Mari. But neither did Zimri-Lim submit to Ibal-pi-El II. He counted on support from his father-in-law, the powerful king of Yamkhad in northern Syria, to remain independent, and informed the latter that he would not make an alliance with Eshnunna. He directed his envoy in Aleppo:

When you find yourself in the presence of Yarim-Lim (king of Yamkhad) on the way to the north, speak to him as follows about Eshnunna: "(The king of) Eshnunna keeps on sending me messages with respect to an alliance. A first time he sent me a messenger and I sent him back at the border. A second time he sent me a messenger and I sent him back at the border. Then a high official came and I sent him back at the border, stating: 'How could I conclude an alliance with Eshnunna without the consent of Yarim-Lim?' "[5]

Although rejected and unable to enforce his wishes immediately, Ibal-pi-El did not withdraw from affairs in the Mari kingdom and Upper Mesopotamia. His relations with Zimri-Lim deteriorated to such an extent that the Mari ruler actively tried to prevent an alliance between Eshnunna and the Syrian city of Qatna.[6]

The excuse to settle scores came from a revolt of the Benjaminite tribesmen against Mari, who from the start of Zimri-Lim's reign had caused a lot of trouble, and had resisted his attempts to control their territories. In 1771, these tribes appealed to Eshnunna for support and Ibal-pi-El obliged by sending out two armies, one into northern Mesopotamia, the other directly to Mari. The threat pushed Zimri-Lim to look for allies and this time Hammurabi responded. A report to the Mari king states:

I have received a message from Abi-mekim in Babylon: "The army of Babylon has started to march." The meals and provisions for these troops are available. I am prepared. The palace and the storehouses are in good shape.[7]

Much of the fighting went on in the north where the rulers of small states were forced to switch allegiance or be summarily replaced by the great powers. The details are very confusing and most of the time they do not involve Babylon directly. But Hammurabi's importance was certainly acknowledged by all, and he was a coveted ally. For example, Zaziya, a ruler from the Zagros mountains who wanted to go to battle against the troops of Eshnunna, declared at some point:

I will have the omens read, and if they are favorable, I will attack the ruler of Eshnunna. If they are unfavorable I will not attack, and write to Hammurabi. Support troops from Babylon will come and Zimri-Lim will arrive, and then we will attack.[8]

The military actions were inconclusive, and in the end Eshnunna was able only to force a weak treaty on Zimri-Lim: the ruler of Eshnunna was in charge but he could demand only minor concessions from Zimri-Lim. The kings themselves did not undertake the negotiations, nor did they ever meet in person. Zimri-Lim had to send a delegation of servants, standards, and divine statues or symbols to Eshnunna to make official his oath to the treaty. His representative wrote: "Now, my Lord had sent his gods, his great standards, and us, his servants, to his father to swear an oath and to bind the hems of father and son for eternity."[9] The language indicates that Eshnunna was the superior power: Ibal-pi-El was the father, Zimri-Lim the son. The tablet with the treaty text is preserved, but it is very fragmentary. Although the treaty forced Zimri-Lim to support Eshnunna's troops by not revealing its plans or aiding its enemies, the other terms were not very arduous. In the end, Eshnunna did not gain any territory in the Euphrates valley, and Mari retained the region to its south.

Meanwhile, Babylon received Mankisum, the city on the Tigris that controlled access from the Diyala into Babylonia, an arrangement certainly imposed by the *sukkal* of Elam, who from his powerful position in the background did not want any single Mesopotamian state to become too strong.

As mentioned in an earlier chapter, it was the ruler of Elam who ended Eshnunna's independence. In 1767, he initiated diplomatic contacts with Mari and Babylon, and in late 1766 or early 1765 this coalition turned against Eshnunna under Elam's leadership. Ibal-pi-El II disappeared from the scene and his capital was raided. Before that moment many cities of his state had temples and palaces where archival texts were written. Afterwards writing in these cities decreased to a trickle, which suggests that the region went into economic decline. The ruler of Elam stayed in the area, however, and instated some new officials. One local north Mesopotamian ruler, Atamrum, became viceroy of Eshnunna and in this way the mighty kingdom lost its freedom.

This situation did not last long. As noted before, Hammurabi dislodged the *sukkal* from the region in 1764, with Zimri-Lim's help and by taking advantage of the resentment of Eshnunna generals. Hammurabi failed to take immediate advantage of this, however. A letter from Zimri-Lim urged the Babylonian to become king of Eshnunna himself, or, if the population would resist, to appoint a local nobleman to represent him:

If the noblemen of Eshnunna allow you, exercise kingship over Eshnunna yourself. If they don't allow you, install a member of the royal family who has lived with you as their king.[10]

For once Hammurabi blundered. Instead of determining who would be king, he permitted the local army to select one of their own. Not only was the new ruler not an appointee of Hammurabi, even worse, he claimed full independence from Babylon. A Mari official reported this to his master:

Eshnunna's army has chosen its own king, and the man they have selected is a commoner. He is not of the royal family. He is called Silli-Sin and he was a military commander. I have heard people say: "This man has become master of the throne and has to govern our country." This is what I heard about Eshnunna.[11]

It was highly unusual in this or any other period of Mesopotamian history for a commoner to rise to kingship, although it is not surprising that it was a military man since the army was so central in the political affairs of the time. Once on the throne, Silli-Sin behaved as a regular king in all respects. A small number of records dated with his year-names show him to have control over the entire state as it existed in Eshnunna's heyday. He appointed officials who declared themselves to be his servants in the seals they used, including men who had served under Ibal-pi-El. A man called Kuzzi, son of Nurri, who had earlier used a seal where he called himself servant of Ibal-pi-El, now had a new one cut, in which he declared allegiance to Silli-Sin.[12] Silli-Sin also restored the palace at Eshnunna, commemorating this work with a short inscription.[13]

Hammurabi was not happy with the situation, but was uncertain how to deal with it. On the one hand, he now sought to patch up relations with Elam, perhaps in order to recapture Eshnunna. On the other hand, he tried to create an alliance with Silli-Sin so that he could focus on Larsa, whose conquest he had begun to plan. He seemingly pursued the latter initiative most seriously. Soon after his accession, Silli-Sin sent messengers to Babylon where they were well received. A Mari letter states:

This man was sent as envoy from Eshnunna to Hammurabi. After he arrived in Babylon, Hammurabi released the Eshnunnean messengers and soldiers he held prisoner, but he still has limited their movements inside the city.[14]

Silli-Sin started the negotiations for a treaty. Yarim-Addu reported these events to his master Zimri-Lim:

I have written to my Lord about the instructions regarding the ruler of Eshnunna that Hammurabi issued . . . When Hammurabi was in the city Borsippa, messengers of Eshnunna's ruler came to him, but he did not see them immediately. Only on the second day they met with him. After having them wait another night, he gave an answer to their report. He gave instructions to [Sin-], son of Kakkarukkum and Mar[duk-mushallim, son of], and he sent them along. They took with them a small tablet (i.e., draft treaty), and they will make the ruler of Eshnunna accept it. (broken word) will go and Hammurabi will accept it. After they will have accepted the small tablet, Hammurabi will send a large tablet, that is a treaty tablet, to the ruler of Eshnunna and make him swear to it. The ruler of Eshnunna will send the large tablet, the treaty tablet, back to Hammurabi and they will establish an alliance. The alliance between Hammurabi and the ruler of Eshnunna is concluded or will be so very soon, that is certain. At this moment the answer to the diplomatic mission of Sin-[ ] and Marduk-mushallim has not yet arrived from Eshnunna. I cannot report on it for my Lord. After this letter I will write to my Lord all the news that reaches me from Eshnunna.[15]

The small tablet mentioned here was a draft treaty, which Hammurabi sent to the king of Eshnunna for his approval before the final treaty was composed. That final step did not seem to materialize fast enough, however, as Silli-Sin repeatedly refused to accept Hammurabi's terms. In a slightly later letter, the same Yarim-Addu reported to Zimri-Lim: "Regarding the small treaty tablet that Hammurabi previously sent to the king of Eshnunna, Silli-Sin: Silli-Sin continues to answer with a refusal and he has not concluded a treaty with Hammurabi."[16] Perhaps this was due to Hammurabi's duplicity since the same letter describes how his envoys to Elam were sneaking through Eshnunna's territory:

I have written earlier to my Lord that the words of Hammurabi were two-faced. Hammurabi has renewed frank conversations with the ruler of Elam as he did before. Elamite messengers who have come from the ruler of Elam to Hammurabi are staying at the entrance of his palace right now. After the ruler of Elam had given them his instructions they were escorted from Susa to Der of the god Ishtaran. The man of Der received them and has sent them under escort to

Malgium, and the man of Malgium was supposed to give them an escort to Babylon. But the army of Eshnunna barred their way and they were unable to enter (the territory). Hammurabi heard that the army of Eshnunna blocked the roads. He no longer sends regular missions to Elam via Malgium and Der, as he did before. But there are open areas in the land Eshnunna and his couriers go to the ruler of Elam through these areas. The message from the ruler of Elam has not yet reached him.[17]

These uncertainties seem to have continued until late in the year 1764. In the end, Hammurabi's overtures to Elam were unsuccessful, and Eshnunna became his ally. A year-name of Silli-Sin is called "The year that Silli-Sin (married) the daughter of Hammurabi," so a diplomatic marriage was concluded in this way. This allowed Hammurabi to engage the bulk of his army in the conquest of Larsa, which he accomplished in 1763.

Even while they were jointly laying siege to Larsa, relations between Babylon and Mari started to cool. As the strongest king of Mesopotamia, Hammurabi became increasingly drawn into the local squabbles in the north as he was asked to help a particular side. For example, Atamrum, the earlier viceroy in Eshnunna who had survived politically by shifting sides from Elam to Mari, wanted Hammurabi's support for his new rule as king of Allahad. So he personally went to Hammurabi during the siege of Larsa and obtained 6,000 Babylonian soldiers. The increased influence of Hammurabi in the north was at the expense of Zimri-Lim, who wanted to dissolve his alliance with Babylon and retrieve control over many of his troops. For both parties, Eshnunna presented a useful ally. Hammurabi's daughter was married to Silli-Sin, but Zimri-Lim sought that king's support as well and was willing to accept his nominal sovereignty. A letter of the official Manatân to Zimri-Lim, who was away from Mari, reported that an embassy from Eshnunna had arrived with gold, silver, and presents.[18] Mari replied in kind: the final mention of Silli-Sin known so far is a record of a gift of a golden vase weighing 38 shekels, that is 320 grams. The account is dated to day 6 of the 8th month of 1762, the final year of Eshnunna and four months before the disappearance of Mari itself.[19]

Hammurabi was furious with Zimri-Lim and harshly attacked him in his privy council, as was communicated to the Mari king by his official Yarim-Addu. Hammurabi thus swore revenge against Mari for having submitted to Eshnunna. He decided to get rid of both rivals, and did so in quick succession. He had to reinforce his army, which had lost its Mari contingents, and did so by enlisting men from the newly conquered territory of Larsa. Still in existence is a very long census list with the names of textile workers recorded late in 1762: some 360 men were accounted for.[20] We can imagine that other professional groups were likewise assessed to determine how many soldiers they could provide.

Hammurabi first turned against Silli-Sin of Eshnunna. Both sides started the usual diplomatic games in an attempt to weaken the other while gaining allies for themselves. Silli-Sin's actions are the best known to us, as some of his envoys were arrested and interrogated by a Mari official, who reported to his master:

I asked them for news about Eshnunna, and they said: "A group of 12,000 men from Eshnunna went up to the city Shitullum. 6,000 of the men carried grain, the other 6,000 escorted them."

Shitullum controlled a point where the Tigris river could be crossed, and allowed access to the north of Mesopotamia. Silli-Sin clearly wanted to hold on to that city. He also stored great amounts of grain there, which he may have used to bribe the northern kings to remain neutral. There is a break in the letter, and when it picks up again, the report continues:

"Silli-Sin has given an enormous amount of grain to the Elamites. They have to transport it to Diniktum and put it at the disposal of the Elamites." Moreover, they said: "A troop of 10,000 Gutians of the queen of Nawar has left just before the festival of 'the seven of the year,' and set out to Larsa. Also, the Babylonians have raided Malgium and have stolen sheep from the Elamites. Also, Hammurabi is in Sippar." That is the news that these men gave me. I asked them what their orders were, and here is the message they were to bring to Ishme-Dagan and Hammurabi (of Kurda): "Keep Subartu under your control and don't give troops to the prince of Babylon as stipulated in the treaty with him. Send a message to Zimri-Lim of Mari that also he should give none to the prince of Babylon."[21]

The messengers from Eshnunna revealed thus all of their king's plans. First, he tried to keep the Elamites out of the war by offering them large amounts of grain. Then he arranged for a raid into Larsa's territory by 10,000 Gutians, his allies from the mountains who were commanded by a queen. This was probably an attempt to dislodge the newly conquered territory from Hammurabi's control. Finally, he sent out messages to rulers of the north asking them not to fulfill their treaty obligations with Babylon. The Mari king should do the same. Hammurabi's preparations are less clear. It seems that he felt strong enough to raid Elam and he did not loose control over Larsa.

The details of the war are almost fully unknown. During the attack on the capital Eshnunna or soon after its capture, Hammurabi sent some 2,700 copper axes and spades from Larsa to the land of Eshnunna, which may have weighed over a ton-and-a-half. The use of these objects is not indicated in the record that documents the shipment: they could have helped the soldiers in the siege, but also may have allowed them to harvest the crops.[22] Agricultural produce was often the main asset of a region, and the large number of soldiers fighting for Hammurabi needed to be fed somehow. It was logical that the local crops were used for that purpose. The substantial number of tools shows that the war was a major operation, and at the end of the year 1762, that is Hammurabi's thirty-first and Zimri-Lim's thirteenth and final year, Hammurabi could proclaim that "he overthrew in battle the army of Eshnunna, Subartu, and Gutium." The combination of hostile forces was the same as those he confronted two years earlier when expelling Elam from Eshnunna, except for the Elamite contingents. He defeated thus all the armies

Silli-Sin could command, that is, from Eshnunna, the Zagros mountains, and northern Mesopotamia.

The consequences of Eshnunna's defeat are wrapped in mystery. Silli-Sin disappeared from the scene but that may be mostly a result of the fact that the Mari archives ended only four months later. Our main source of information on international affairs was suddenly terminated. In Eshnunna's territory only a few records dated to Silli-Sin's reign were found, and it is unclear when exactly his rule ended, immediately after Hammurabi defeated him or later. Nor do records dated with Hammurabi's year-names replace those of a local Eshnunna ruler. The only written evidence of Hammurabi's presence in the region consists of two bronze knobs, found on a site in a suburb of modern Baghdad, inscribed with the sentence "palace of Hammurabi."[23] He seems thus to have had an official residence in Eshnunna territory close to the border with Babylonia, but is unlikely to have fully incorporated Eshnunna into his kingdom. The year-name that announces Eshnunna's defeat states also that Hammurabi annexed Mankisum, the crucial point where one crosses the Tigris between Babylonia and Eshnunna, and that area was probably both the focus of his attention and the extent of his control. In later years Eshnunna seems to have continued to resist Babylon, forcing Hammurabi to return there with his army in 1756. His thirty-eighth year-name states that "he destroyed Eshnunna with a great flood." The interpretation of that statement is not self-evident, but it may indicate that he undermined the city walls by diverting rivers and canals to engulf them. Such a tactic was applied elsewhere in Mesopotamian history. It is possible that Eshnunna rebelled after it lost its independence in 1762, and that in 1756 Hammurabi punished the capital city for that behavior. A similar sequence of events took place in Mari.

Archaeological exploration indicates that the lower Diyala region went through an economic decline as a result of Hammurabi's military actions. People abandoned the cities and went to live in villages. The reduced political and economic circumstances of the region continued after Hammurabi's death. Some local Eshnunnean rulers are attested, but with only scanty evidence. Their independence may have annoyed the rulers of Babylon, and Hammurabi's successor, Samsuiluna, claims to have conquered the entire region, turning one of the old cities, Tutub, into a fortress named after him, Dur-Samsuiluna. The region did not go into full decline, however, as some of its settlements continued their existence from the seventeenth century into the fifteenth without interruption. Babylon's campaigns did not, then, create a scorched landscape.

The actions of Hammurabi toward Eshnunna had a logical premise. He could not allow the state to exist as a major power on his northern border. Not only did it block his access to regions further north in Mesopotamia, but as a strong power it threatened some of his important cities, such as Sippar which was only twenty kilometers from the border with Eshnunna. The drive to eliminate Eshnunna took longer than expected, because the removal of Elam in 1764 did not lead to Hammurabi having full control over the region. Local forces were still too strong and Silli-Sin was a powerful opponent. Hammurabi needed to wait until he got rid of Larsa before he could attack Eshnunna. He did not annex its territory but got free access to the regions of northern Mesopotamia, since the Tigris corridor was now in his hands. There was thus an opening for further conquests.

5

Supremacy in the North

At the same time that Hammurabi celebrated his defeat of
Eshnunna in 1762, he claimed to have overcome the army of
Subartu and to have conquered the lands along the Tigris river
"up to the frontier of the land of Subartu." Subartu had been
an ally of Elam when Hammurabi had defeated that state in
1764, and it appears as an opponent in later years as well. The
term Subartu does not seem to refer to a specific kingdom,
but the Babylonians used it to indicate "the north of Mesopotamia" in general. In it was a patchwork of small states
whose number is unclear. A profusion of names of such states
appears in Hammurabi's official statements, such as Ekallatum,
Zalmaqum, Burunda, Kakmum, and Turukkum. Their histor-
ies, and often even locations, are little-known to us, and they
were probably vague to the Babylonians as well. These states
were not formidable opponents to the now mighty Hammurabi,
nor was their conquest his aim. But he was drawn into their
squabbles when some requested his military support, and he
may have wanted to "pacify" the region to end the instability
their infighting generated. In the end, this allowed him to
impose his wishes on the affairs of the region, although he
never truly incorporated northern Mesopotamia into the
Babylonian state.

The fragmentation of power in northern Mesopotamia was
so great that strong armies, such as Hammurabi's, could reach
through to distant places seemingly without much resistance.

Thus we find Babylon's troops suddenly near the modern Turkish border or in the Zagros mountains on what seem to have been quick raids. They encountered no strong adversaries, but also seem not to have been intent on drastically changing the political scene. The history of northern Mesopotamia is exceedingly complicated because so many actors were involved, some of whom were very shifty characters in diplomatic terms, switching allegiance and attacking former friends. Hammurabi remained an outsider to them, only the latest in a series of powerful Near Eastern rulers whose support was craved by the various parties and who were able to dictate what happened for a time.

Northern Mesopotamia was a vast expanse, roughly a triangle of some 500 by 300 by 500 kilometers, bounded by the Taurus and Zagros mountains in the north and east, and by the Euphrates river with the Syrian desert beyond in the west. It contained a great variety of natural environments: lush mountain valleys; wide plains where rainfall supported crops; harsh and arid steppe-lands; and narrow river valleys with irrigation agriculture in the lowlands. The people in the area lived similarly differing lifestyles. Some resided in villages, farming the surrounding fields, others moved with their herds of sheep and goats through the steppe, sometimes at great distances from settlements, and yet others lived in cities. There were few cities in northern Mesopotamia that could claim the antiquity of Babylonian cities; such as could were located mostly in the Tigris and Euphrates valleys. The region was at the end of a very prosperous period in its history, however, and several urban centers had been founded across the land in the first centuries of the second millennium. Those were the seats of the royal houses that controlled the immediate surroundings.

During the early years of Hammurabi's reign, Shamshi-Adad had unified much of the north and turned it into the major political power of Mesopotamia. But when he died in 1776, Hammurabi's seventeenth year of rule, his sons were unable to keep the state together. Shamshi-Adad's oldest son,

Ishme-Dagan, held on to the capital, Ekallatum, in the east, but the younger, Yasmah-Addu, was expelled from Mari. In many other cities, descendants of dynasties that had ruled before recovered power as well. These newly independent states did not live peacefully together, however. On the contrary, many of them lobbied for power, attacked and conquered their neighbors, and constantly plotted against others. The powerful neighbors of the bordering regions carefully watched the immensely complex situation, and they were eager to gain some control over it: Yamkhad in the north-west; Mari in the south-west; Eshnunna in the south-east; and Babylon in the south. As the Mari kingdom was the closest neighbor, it felt that it had the right to dictate what happened: Zimri-Lim kept himself well-informed and the letters written to him reveal numerous incidents in great detail. Most of these did not involve Hammurabi directly, who only entered the region with his troops after the final defeat of Eshnunna in 1762. Years before that, however, his increased status in the whole region made him a sought-after ally. Thus his presence can be observed in the background off and on, when local rulers solicited his support. There are several examples of this, and we will look here at the case of Ishme-Dagan, who repeatedly relied on Babylon for his survival. His relationship with the king of Babylon vacillated enormously: one day he was a good friend and trusted ally, the next he was a small-time vassal who had to know his place. Hammurabi knew he could play with him, as Ishme-Dagan's survival as king seems to have depended on Babylon's support. He could adapt his demeanor to the northern king thus according to his needs of the day.

When Shamshi-Adad's kingdom of Upper Mesopotamia dissolved into a patchwork of small states in 1776, his son Ishme-Dagan remained ruler only of Ekallatum, the dynastic seat. We do not know how much territory he controlled. Of the first twelve years of his reign we know little, but this changed when Elam entered the region of northern Mesopotamia and occupied several states there. Because Ishme-Dagan was

Hammurabi's ally, his local enemies could easily denounce him in front of the ruler of Elam. In a later message to Hammurabi he reminded him of these events:

> I have been in trouble because of my Lord's problems. When the man of Elam was at war with my Lord, kings of the land of Subartu slandered me before the *sukkal* of Elam and took me to Eshnunna. The *sukkal* of Elam cross-examined me and I was only saved because of some help.[1]

Ishme-Dagan may have bribed his way out of this moment of trouble. When, somewhat later, he turned up at Hammurabi's court in Babylon, a diviner accused him of theft from the temple for that purpose. A report to Zimri-Lim of Mari reads:

> The diviner of the god Marduk stood at the palace gate and kept on shouting: "Ishme-Dagan will not escape from the hand of Marduk! His booty will be a sheaf of barley." That is what he kept on shouting and no one said anything to him. Then he went to Ishme-Dagan's door and kept on shouting in the midst of a large crowd: "You have gone to the *sukkal* of Elam to make peace. In order to make peace you have taken to the *sukkal* of Elam treasures that belong to Marduk and the city of Babylon. You have emptied storehouses and magazines that belong to Marduk and have not returned the favors he gave you. And now you want to leave for Ekallatum? He who spends the treasure of Marduk should not expect favors from him!" That is what he kept on shouting in the midst of the people, and no one said anything to him.[2]

Ishme-Dagan had a severe battle wound, which the diviner saw as retribution by Babylon's main god Marduk. The diviner made very serious accusations, among them that Ishme-Dagan had stolen temple treasures to give them to Elam. It is unclear how he would have spirited funds out of Babylon to do so, and the truth of the accusations cannot be confirmed.

Hammurabi was willing to forgive him, however, as Ishme-Dagan's troops were welcome in Babylon's coalition against Elam. He allowed Ishme-Dagan's generals into his secret council meetings, a fact that disturbed Zimri-Lim's representative in

Babylon who had not been accorded such privileges. He wrote to Zimri-Lim:

> The servants of Ishme-Dagan, that is Ishar-Lim, Mutu-Haqim and Rim-Addu, have ousted the lords of the land and they themselves have become the masters of Hammurabi's council. He listens to their advice. Once or twice, when (the diviners) Hali-Hadun and Inib-Shamash read the oracles and reported on them, Ishar-Lim, Mutu-Haqim and Rim-Addu were not asked to leave. As they were present, they heard the message of the oracles. What other secret is there beside the secret report of the diviners? While his own servants do not hear the secrets of the diviners, these men do![3]

He warned that "These men and Ishme-Dagan will cause trouble between Hammurabi and my Lord."[4] Ekallatum did supply troops to Hammurabi in his war against Elam,[5] and Ishme-Dagan stayed in Babylon for at least a couple of months.

In his absence, some people at home, in conjunction with the Elamite general Atamrum, planned to place Ishme-Dagan's son, Mut-Ashkur, on the throne of Ekallatum. But the prince was held prisoner elsewhere, and a huge ransom sum had to be paid:

> 1 gold-plated throne, 2 pedestals, 2 gold-plated tables, 1 sedan-chair made in Aleppo, 1 chariot whose "mane" is gold and whose "horns" are alabaster, 10 gold-plated bronze spears, 40 silver-plated bronze spears, 250 bronze spears, and 50 (broken word), garments and shirts, and 20 servants.[6]

The father managed to get home in time, however, soon after Elam's defeat in 1764, and he reclaimed his throne. The son does not seem to have been punished since many years later he did succeed his father legitimately. Perhaps at the time he was a young boy, chosen by rebels to be placed on the throne while they made all-important decisions behind the scenes. Upon his return Ishme-Dagan immediately got back into the politicking of the time, seeking new friends and making enemies.

His popularity with Hammurabi seems to have waned, however. Early in 1763, his kingdom was attacked once more, and Ishme-Dagan sent another delegation to ask Hammurabi for help. The Babylonian was in the midst of the siege of Larsa, and perhaps less patient with his ally in the distant north, who not only wanted military support, but also respect. The emissaries reminded Hammurabi of Ishme-Dagan's past assistance and then passed on this request for troops:

Zaziya the Turukkean is marching against my country and has seized two or three cities. He is putting pressure on my country. I have written to you regarding troops, but you have not sent me troops, while you have given some to others.

A lively exchange ensued:

Hammurabi replied: "To whom have I given troops? Tell me. Tell me." He repeated his question five or six times and forced them to say: "You have given troops to Atamrum." And Hammurabi answered: "What troops have I given to Atamrum? I have only made three to four hundred men go to him."

Hammurabi said: "You must have some other news." They said: "No. We're not hiding a secret message your servant would have sent. Don't hurt us. Our Lord is like a doormat under your feet. Even if other kings honor you, none write the same messages of submission to you." When Ishme-Dagan's messengers told him that, Hammurabi replied: "As you don't want to complete your message, my servant who has come with you will do so." So Hammurabi fetched his servant who had come with them. After he had repeated the report that the messengers of Ishme-Dagan had given, he completed it: "You make me write to Zimri-Lim as if I am his son, but is he not my servant? He does not sit on a higher throne, so I do not address him with higher greetings."

When Hammurabi heard this, he yelled out: "What a scandal!" The messengers of Ishme-Dagan denied the message: "We were not given such a message at all. After we left, Ili-ite, a servant of Ishme-Dagan, came to us and said: "It is not about my Lord Zimri-Lim that this message was sent, but about Atamrum." Hammurabi said to Ishme-Dagan's messengers: "The kings of Subartu have denounced your master, and I wrote to him as follows: 'To the kings that write to me as sons, you have to write as brothers. To Zimri-Lim who writes to me as a brother, you have to write as a son.' Is there something wrong with what I wrote?"[7]

We get here a rare glimpse of Hammurabi's personality. He was certainly impatient with Ishme-Dagan's men, who were afraid of him and portrayed their own king as a doormat under his feet. They feared to criticize Hammurabi and refused to report their master's complaint that he was not regarded on the same level as Zimri-Lim. Hammurabi did not like to be told how to conduct his business. He claimed the right to determine which king was important, and which one was not. Zimri-Lim was still his equal (he also furnished a large number of troops to help in the siege of Larsa), but Ishme-Dagan was only a petty ruler, who needed to honor the king of Mari.

In practical terms, Hammurabi was not willing to sacrifice troops to shore up Ishme-Dagan's kingship. It was more useful to help out Ishme-Dagan's archenemy, Atamrum, to whom he had sent a small contingent. Diplomacy demanded, however, that he did not admit to this openly. After all, Ishme-Dagan was still a friend and ally. Thus Hammurabi played down the importance of his support to Atamrum: he had sent only three to four hundred men.

Rejected by Hammurabi, Ishme-Dagan was not at a loss, however. He could easily find other allies amongst Hammurabi's enemies, and the king of Eshnunna answered his request for military aid. This allowed Ishme-Dagan to take the offensive against some of his neighbors, including Mari. Not that this protected his home territory. In the hurly-burly of the time, there were always those ready to venture an attack. Zaziya, the king of Turukkum in the Zagros Mountains, played a trick on him, as was reported to Zimri-Lim:

Zaziya proposed peace to Ishme-Dagan, but he set a trap for him. The gods of Ishme-Dagan were with Zaziya, so that he could swear an oath, and his ships were moored at Kawalhum. As soon as Zaziya tricked Ishme-Dagan into that, he sent 3,000 men to the gates of Ekallatum. They killed a hundred people, pillaged, and took away to a place called "The Barn" some one hundred men and women from four villages. They seized flocks of sheep and goats and all that they found on the way to Ekallatum. They left nothing in the country except the city Ekallatum, which, by itself, saved its own skin.[8]

The same letter declared that the Eshnunnean general in the region, supposedly an ally, did nothing to help. So, Ishme-Dagan was in trouble again, and once more he fled to Babylon.

These uncertainties and constant clashes may have exasperated Hammurabi, and forced him the "pacify" the region. In 1762, the year that he sacked Eshnunna, somewhere in the neighborhood of 15,000 to 28,000 of his men were tied down in an occupation of a large stretch of northern Mesopotamia, especially in the northern Tigris valley. There was no full integration of this region into the Babylonian state, however. Ishme-Dagan and many other local rulers stayed in power as petty kings, or were replaced by family members who were considered to be more loyal to Hammurabi.

The conquest of Mari by Hammurabi in 1761 led to a disappearance of the archives that are the chief source of information on the region, and we are much less informed about subsequent years. There are some shreds of evidence, however, that allow us to piece together how Hammurabi dealt with northern Mesopotamia after 1761. Most informative are the archives found in a small city, Qattara, some 100 kilometers north-west of Ekallatum. It was part of a kingdom that had been forced to accept Zimri-Lim's hegemony for many years, but with Hammurabi's ascendancy, King Ashkur-Addu had been removed from the throne. His brother-in-law and military commander, Aqba-Hammu, who was also a diviner, was put in charge. In his official seal he called himself "servant of Hammurabi," clearly indicating his inferior status. Letters to his wife, Iltani, indicate that his emissaries regularly visited and delivered tribute to Babylon. Thus Iltani's son, Re'um-El, wrote to her:

I have arrived safely in Babylon and have seen king Hammurabi in a good mood. I will be back soon after this letter. Be happy.[9]

Aqba-Hammu was responsible for the rather substantial tribute of the state. In one letter he wrote to his wife:

I will bring many textiles to Babylon as my tribute . . . Send me as many as there are soon. I have collected all the textiles that are available here, but those are not enough.[10]

He may have been forced to bring the tribute personally as a sign of submission.

Hammurabi needed to intimidate rebellious kings once in a while, and Babylonian troop movements were of concern to the locals. At one point Aqba-Hammu wrote to Iltani:

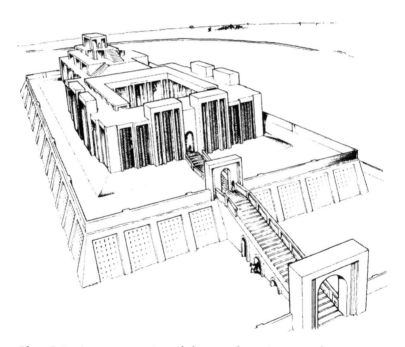

Plate 5.1 A reconstruction of the temple at Qattara. This was the main temple of the city at the time of its interactions with Hammurabi (from S. Dalley, *Mari and Karana*. London: Longman, 1984, fig. 36; courtesy S. Dalley)

Tell Iltani, Aqba-Hammu says: You wrote to me about the 1,000 troops that came up from Babylon and have entered the city Andarig. Why did your servant who brought the news not (broken word), and why did you not ask him for a full account? Send him to me, so that I can ask him for a full account.[11]

Military actions of this type must have been the basis of Hammurabi's claims in later year-names that he defeated armies of northern states. Such declarations are found up to his thirty-ninth year when he claims to have slaughtered the enemies of the Subartu mountains.

The north would not remain under Babylon's control for long. Hammurabi's successor Samsuiluna was unable to fully dominate the region, but neither did he entirely neglect it. In 1728, he even marched all the way up to Shubat-Enlil, Shamshi-Adad's ancient capital, and sacked it. This was the end of a long period of slow decline of the region, which had changed from a realm of densely-inhabited, wealthy cities to one with only a few remaining outposts. Only centuries later would this northern world thrive anew.

6

The Sack of Mari

Almost all the information about Hammurabi's military and diplomatic activities in the second half of his reign comes from the palace archives of Mari. The ruler of that city, Zimri-Lim, was Hammurabi's ally in several wars and kept well apprised of the actions of his Babylonian colleague. The alliance between the two was very fragile, however. It was based on a shared interest in removing still other kings from the political scene, and it only loosely papered over the fact that Babylon and Mari were also competitors and suspicious of one another. In the end, their alliance collapsed and they turned against each other. When Hammurabi won the war and sacked Mari, he not only completed his project of annihilating his neighbors, but coincidentally also terminated the archives that so vividly described his actions. When Mari officials stopped writing to their master, we become ignorant about Babylon's subsequent international affairs.

By the eighteenth century, Mari was an ancient city, already some 700 years old, that derived its prominence from its strategic location at the middle of the Euphrates river valley. The narrow valley provided the only summer grazing to herdsmen, who moved around the Syrian steppe during the winter when the desert blooms. The migration into Mari's territory enabled that city to control the pastoral people and thus indirectly the wide zone between Mesopotamia and the fertile lands along the Mediterranean. Moreover, the trade route from Babylonia to north-west Syria and the Mediterranean coast beyond had to run by Mari, which controlled thus the juncture between Mesopotamia and the west. This explains why, from the mid-third millennium on, Mari had been in close contact with Babylonia and shared many Babylonian cultural elements, while at the same time also being part of the Syrian political and cultural area. It was a true gateway between the two regions.

Because of its strategic location, Shamshi-Adad used Mari as one of the three capitals of his kingdom of Upper Mesopotamia and placed his younger son, Yasmah-Addu, on the throne there. Yasmah-Addu's role was to oversee the tribesmen of the Syrian desert and to deal with the affairs of the western part of the kingdom. When his father died, the local population quickly removed him, and a new ruler, Zimri-Lim, seized the throne. That man's ancestry is somewhat mysterious: often he presented himself as the son of Yahdun-Lim, the last ruler of Mari before Shamshi-Adad's take-over. But in reality he was the son of another man, Hadni-Addu, a member of the powerful Sim'alite tribes of northern Syria. Zimri-Lim was thus one of the several men with tribal roots who took control over ancient urban centers in a time of great political confusion, integrating themselves into the local dynastic tradition.

Zimri-Lim soon adjusted to his role as an urban king, however, and set himself up in Mari's palace, which was internationally famous for its beauty in those days. He controlled the middle Euphrates valley from the border with Babylonia, 200 kilometers to its south, to the border with the kingdom of Yamkhad 250 kilometers to the north. The lands in the Habur river valley provided him with a rich agricultural area. He exercised a lot of power throughout northern Mesopotamia, either directly or through vassals. Since the latter switched political sides regularly, the area under his control often changed extent. He certainly belonged, however, to the league of great kings of the time, including Hammurabi of Babylon, Ibal-pi-El of Eshnunna, and Rim-Sin of Larsa. Since they were

Plate 6.1   Aerial view of the palace at Mari. This view, taken
during the excavations in the 1930s, shows the enormous extent of
the palace and its elaborate layout. In its rooms the international
correspondence of the Mari kings was excavated (© Mission
archéologique de Mari; courtesy J.-Cl. Margueron)

neighbors, Zimri-Lim's contacts with Hammurabi were close,
although it seems that the two men never met in person.
Instead, high officials moved back and forth between the two
courts. Among those were the sons of Hammurabi, who were
regularly at Zimri-Lim's court or in other cities of his kingdom. Suitable housing had to be found for them, which sometimes forced people to give up their homes. A letter from the
city Terqa to Zimri-Lim dealt with such a matter:

Concerning the house of Aqba-ahum I keep on hearing: "The son of
Hammurabi will stay in that house." But the things of Aqba-ahum
and his people have not yet been removed. Or perhaps it is not
needed. My Lord should let me know what he wants, one way or
another, so that there is no unhappiness. Does Aqba-ahum have to
leave the house? In any case, my Lord should write to me. Servants
should arrive fast to clear out the people and their things.[1]

Even the crown prince, Sumuditana, visited Mari shortly before the two states became hostile.

The balance of power that existed in Mesopotamia in the first half of Hammurabi's reign was partly maintained by the tacit agreement that all kings in the region accepted the superiority of the king of Elam. As a distant, yet very powerful, ruler, he was asked to settle disputes and his authority was acknowledged by all. For example, the king of Elam had ruled that Hit, a city on the Euphrates, would be the property of Mari. Hammurabi did not like that decision at all. The disagreement over Hit would hang over his relations with Zimri-Lim, causing ill feeling between the two kings while they still needed each other's help.

Hit was located on the border between the kingdoms of Mari and Babylon, and was rich in bitumen, which Hammurabi needed to caulk his boats. On the other hand, for Mari, Hit had a totally different importance: it was the place where a special judicial activity took place, the river ordeal. People who were accused of various crimes, including adultery and sorcery, or who had competing claims over a property, were taken to the Euphrates to establish the validity of their declarations. The river was considered to be a divine judge. The accused or claimant had to swear to a statement, and one or more persons (not necessarily the accused but often a replacement) had to jump into the water to find out the river's verdict. A difficult task was set. For example, a millstone had to be taken across the river, or a certain distance had to be swum under the water. When the person re-emerged too soon, or drowned, the oath was considered false. A letter to Zimri-Lim describes the practice in some detail:

Concerning the people who had to submit to the river-ordeal on account of Shubram and Haya-Sumu, whom my Lord sent, I sent comptrollers with this group. First, they made a woman jump in the water, and she came up immediately. Then they made an old man jump. After swimming a distance of 80 measures in the divine river, he saved himself and came up. After him, they made a second woman go down, and she came up immediately. After her, a third woman, and she drowned. Because the old man only swam 80 measures and the third woman drowned, the people of Haya-Sumu refused to let the last three women jump. They attested: "The settlement and the fields do not belong to us." The old man threw himself before the feet of the people of Shubram and said: "Don't make the remaining women jump. They may die! We will write a tablet that we don't claim the city and the fields. No one will ever in the future contest that the city and the fields belong to Shubram." They had such a tablet composed before the comptrollers, the Babylonian attendants, and the city-elders. I will send the people who had to jump to my Lord, so that he can question them.[2]

The town of Hit was the preferred place for this type of test, and it was also referred to as the "City of the River Ordeal." Not only Mari used it, but people from as far as Aleppo and Elam visited it as well. This juridical and religious import- ance may have been the reason why Zimri-Lim was so attached to Hit, and why he wanted to keep full control over the city.

The negotiations over the city started in 1770, but did not go well at all. Hammurabi put pressure on Zimri-Lim, whose advisors told him not to give in. The official in charge of Hit wrote to Zimri-Lim:

My Lord has communicated to me the content of the tablet that Hammurabi, king of Babylon, sent him. This Hammurabi exaggerates so much, and he lies! My Lord will see that. Doesn't my Lord know that Hammurabi, king of Babylon, will conclude an alliance with him?[3]

The letter writer urged a skeptical attitude toward Hammurabi and suggested that Zimri-Lim resist pressure on the matter of Hit since Hammurabi badly needed an alliance with Mari. This was an accurate analysis, but the issue was too important to both men to be delayed, and before long two messengers to Babylon reported this long exchange to Zimri-Lim:

We arrived in Sippar-the-great and Yansib-Addu, my Lord's servant, delivered his message to Hammurabi. While Yansib-Addu delivered the message, Hammurabi was (broken word) and for the entire time he listened and did not open his mouth. When the message was finished, he spoke to us: "Since the beginning of time, has this house done anything wrong to Mari and has there ever been conflict between Mari and Babylon? Since the beginning of time, Mari and Babylon have been like a single house and a single finger, without any war cries. And now Zimri-Lim gives me full reports and speaks openly to me, while before his father and grandfather did not do so. From the moment Zimri-Lim has turned to me and has started to correspond with me, there has been no evil or aggression against him from my part. I have done everything good possible for him, and he knows the good I have done."

He said that and many other good things. I answered him: "You have done nothing wrong to my Lord, and he has done nothing wrong to you. You have done everything good possible to my Lord, and he has done everything good possible to you. He has honored and praised you. Among all the allied kings whose words you transmit and whose greetings you send to the *sukkal* of Elam, there is no one who has treated you so well and has honored you as much. Upon your request he arrested the messengers of Eshnunna, and sent them to you. Moreover, when you asked him to send troops, my Lord selected the best troops to send to you. You know how I have told not once or five times, but many times: 'Even if you would no longer accept my Lord's messages despite his repeated writing, and if my Lord would lose favor with you, know well who my Lord really is, and that he would do good things for you.' I kept on repeating to you for a long time: 'Don't you see what my Lord wants?' Now, in exchange for the good my Lord has done for you and the way he has honored you, give him satisfaction and come to an agreement regarding the cities that the *sukkal* of Elam, your father, has given to him, and may all be done in honesty."

I told him that and he replied: "Among the allied kings there is indeed no one who has treated me as well and has honored me like Zimri-Lim. For all the good he has done for me, I will give him satisfaction, and an eternal bond will be established between us. Make clear your concerns, so that I can answer." I said: "You should be the one who makes things clear," and he said: "I will. Give the names of the cities that I should agree on." I said: "Hit, Harbu, and Yabliya," and he said: "Don't mention Hit. In the past Shamshi-Adad took away Rapiqum from Eshnunna and gave it to me. Since then my troops have been there and they are still there. In those days Shamshi-Adad's troops resided there as well. Now Zimri-Lim's reside there. Just as mine and his troops are together (at Rapiqum) they can be together (at Hit). May an eternal peace exist between us."[4]

The exchange indicates that Hammurabi was unwilling to give up his claim, although Zimri-Lim was a good and trusted ally. He urged his colleague to share power in Hit as they had done in Rapiqum. He could not press his claim too hard, since Elam was still the greatest power in the region and had ruled in Mari's favor. But that changed when Elam's friendly relations with Babylon and Mari ended and hostilities erupted in 1765. The impending war against Elam gave Hammurabi an opening to reject its earlier decision, but he was confronted with a dilemma. On the one hand, he was eager to press Mari on the matter of Hit; on the other hand he needed Mari as an ally against Elam. Two tracks of negotiations were thus opened at the same time. The conclusion of an alliance against Elam was discussed in chapter 2: Mari had been reluctant to cut its ties with Elam, but went over to Hammurabi's camp after its own northern territories were threatened by that country. Both kings swore an oath to an anti-Elam treaty, and the two armies joined forces.

As a reward for his support, Zimri-Lim wanted a settlement on Hit, and he asked Hammurabi to withdraw his claims. He sent Abi-mekim to Babylon with a draft treaty. The emissary reported back:

My Lord's mission is going well. I arrived in Babylon and related to Hammurabi the message my Lord gave me. He was happy and stated: "It must have been at a god's command that Zimri-Lim sent me these words. Now that I, Zimri-Lim and Yarim-Lim (Zimri-Lim's father-in-law and king of Yamkhad) have concluded an alliance, and we have joined forces, no enemy or foe can do anything and we will remove the enemy's grip from this land." Hammurabi said this and other things and he was in a good mood. I told him everything to make him feel good and I pleased him with my words.

On the second day, I brought to him the treaty tablet that my Lord had drafted. He listened to it but when Hammurabi heard what was in the treaty about Yumahammu, Hit and Yabliya, he said: "Why does Zimri-Lim create difficulties despite his good words? Why did he write the cities of Yumahammu and Hit on the treaty tablet and send it to me?" I answered: "Never has my Lord laid claim to something that does not belong to him."[5]

The next passage of the letter is damaged. When it becomes legible again, Hammurabi declared:

"Take Hit out of the treaty text, so that I can swear to it. Then go to your troops and start the campaign. After our goal has been reached, our fellow kings will come together and judge this matter. I will accept their verdict."

He told me that and I replied: "My Lord has gathered for you the support of the entire country, and he has marched against the evil enemy, who surrounded you, to defeat him and remove his grip from the land of Akkad. In return for all the good things my Lord has done, withdraw your claim on the cities that belong to my Lord and swear by the river-god. Do him a favor and when all is well and over, do not bring up this subject of disagreement again and start trouble." He answered: "I told you my concerns . . . Why do I want Hit? Your country's power lies in donkeys and chariots. My country's power lies in ships. That is exactly why I really want the bitumen and pitch from that city. Why else would I want the city from him? In return for Hit, I will listen to anything Zimri-Lim asks."[6]

The economic importance of Hit for Hammurabi is thus clear: his boats that transport goods and people over rivers and canals had to be waterproofed with bitumen. In Hammurabi's view, that was not a concern for Zimri-Lim whose people used chariots for transport.

The need for soldiers made Hammurabi eager to conclude a treaty, but he did not want to give up Hit so he tried to postpone the argument. Meanwhile, Zimri-Lim had the same predicament: he needed troops against Elam, which had occupied parts of northern Mesopotamia, and he considered surrendering Hit. At one point he consulted one of his diviners:

Take emergency oracles about the yielding of Hit to the king of Babylon. Ask: "Should Zimri-Lim yield Hit to the king of Babylon? Would he be safe? Would his country be well and flourish?"[7]

The diviner cut open two lambs asking the question whether Zimri-Lim should relent, and the answer was unfavorable. To confirm the answer, he asked then whether Zimri-Lim should not relent, and the oracle concurred.

Despite the lack of progress in the negotiations, Abi-mekim was able to get troops from Hammurabi, at the same time that Zimri-Lim sent military support to Babylon. This exchange of men may be more an indication of how they mistrusted one another than of their friendship. Both kings held a contingent of the other hostage, which gave some guarantee that the other would not cheat and turn to the enemy.

Even during their cooperation the kings were highly suspicious of one another. Troop movements occurred all over the region and allies of Babylon, for example, could feel threatened by Zimri-Lim's army. Hammurabi himself did not like the fact that Zimri-Lim had assembled a large army in the north to face Eshnunna's general Atamrum. At one point he received a report that Yamkhad and Zalmaqum in northern Syria had sent troops to Zimri-Lim:

10,000 men of Yamkhad just left Tuttul, and they expect 10,000 men from Zalmaqum. They are going to Ida-maras to confront Atamrum.[8]

Hammurabi complained to Zimri-Lim's envoy when he heard this:

I have learned that Zimri-Lim intends to go to Ida-maras. In reality he wants to march against me! He has plotted as follows: "I have to prevent that, when an army from Qatna goes to Hammurabi, he would have more troops than I do, and people would say 'Zimri-Lim has no allies.' "[9]

Both kings had thus little confidence in one another, but their armies fought side by side for about two years in the wars against Elam and Larsa. Even before they triumphed over Larsa, Zimri-Lim was desperate for the return of his men to be used in his wars in the north. He also needed help and asked Hammurabi for extra troops. But Hammurabi was reluctant to commit any men, even those from Mari itself. He tried to delay:

"Yes, today or very soon, I will send a heavily armed army to your master, and he will be able to attain his goal." That is what Hammurabi keeps on telling us, but we said: "Even before you take Larsa and you can send a heavily armed army to your brother, you, our Lord, should send a group of 2,000, even only 1,000, men to your brother, if only so that the allies can hear: "The Babylonian army has arrived." With great difficulty and after lots of talking, he agreed with us to let go 1,000 men under these conditions: "In five days I will have seen the fate of the city. If the city resists, I will send your master a group of 1,000 men, but if the city is taken I will send a (larger) group of men." This is what Hammurabi answered.[10]

The same discussion is reported to Zimri-Lim by at least two more officials, which shows how important the issue was to him. Hammurabi did not fulfill his promise, it seems, and he only reluctantly let even Mari's own army go back home, after the conquest and pacification of Larsa.

Simultaneously, both kings had initiated secret contacts with the new king of Eshnunna, Silli-Sin, and they were willing to break their mutual treaty if they could get his support. While they were still in Larsa, Zimri-Lim's envoy dared to point out to Hammurabi how misguided and poorly timed an alliance with Eshnunna would be:

Fine. If it turns out that the god has created a friendship between you and the man of Eshnunna, what are your brother's (i.e., Zimri-Lim's) servants doing here? If the god, after creating this friendship (i.e., between Babylon and Eshnunna), allows a transgression of the treaty, what could you do about it now, that is in the middle of the winter? Would you lay siege to the city (i.e., Eshnunna) or raid its country?[11]

Being courted by both kings, Silli-Sin of Eshnunna was careful. He had married the daughter of Hammurabi, but also concluded a treaty with Zimri-Lim. The latter made Hammurabi furious at Zimri-Lim. In his opinion, the Mari ruler had broken his oath and had become an enemy: "Since he has seized the hem of the robe of Eshnunna's ruler, I want to make him pay for it."[12] To counter this alliance, Hammurabi started negotiations with Elam, bribed Malgium, and sought

northern allies, such as Ishme-Dagan of Ekallatum and others.
When he managed to conquer Eshnunna in 1762, and had
large armies in the north, he cut off most support from Zimri-
Lim, and had the free hand he needed to attack this final
major competitor.

Years before, the Mari king had bribed Babylonians to
spy on Hammurabi and communicate the discussions of the
secret council to him, so he must have been well-informed.
He was cautious, however, and wanted divine assurance. So
he asked his wife, Shibtu, to consult the oracles:

Ask the oracles about Hammurabi of Babylon. Will this man ever
die? Does he speak honestly with us? Will he declare war? Will he
start a siege when I am on campaign in the north? Ask questions
about that man. When you have done the questioning once, repeat it
and write me all the answers to your questions.[13]

Shibtu did write back:

I have asked my questions about Babylon. That man is plotting many
things against this country, but he will not succeed. My Lord will
see what the god will do to him. You will capture and overpower
him. His days are numbered and he will not live long. My Lord
should know![14]

Others were equally optimistic. The then-famous oracle of
Dagan at Tuttul declared, "O Babylon, what are you doing?
I will capture you with a sword and battle net. I will give the
palaces of your seven conspirators and their treasures all to
Zimri-Lim."[15]

The oracles were terribly wrong. Hammurabi started a
two-pronged attack on Mari, from the south and the north.
Zimri-Lim received this report about the southern advance:

Hammura[ ] and Dada[ ], the generals, and Kakkarukkum, the diviner,
are the three officers that head an army of 4,000 heavily equipped
men. We have left Babylon three days before I sent this tablet to my
Lord. In four days the army will approach Hanat. Let my Lord make
arrangements.[16]

Hanat was on the border of Zimri-Lim's territory and only a two-day march from Mari itself. The first general's name in this message is not fully preserved, but chances are great that it was Hammurabi himself. Simultaneously, a Babylonian army of 20,000 men was gathered to the north of Mari, commanded by Mutu-Haqdum and Rim-Addu, two sworn enemies of Mari. While the main body was probably made up of soldiers that were already present in the area because of Hammurabi's earlier campaigns there, reinforcements sneaked through Mari's territory under false pretenses. Hammurabi did not want to show his intentions clearly, it seems. A report to Zimri-Lim suggests this:

Three days before I sent this letter to you, my guards who were scouting warned me: "500 Babylonian soldiers are advancing, carrying the order to go to Ekallatum." When they arrived from Babylon in the area of Sapiratum, my guards interrogated them: "What is your destination?" They answered: "Ekallatum." But when they reached Sapiratum, they left the road to Ekallatum, and took the high road, that is the one on which La-awil-Addu made Issur-Sin, son of Atamrum, go north. Maybe this army is going to Karana or Andarig. I don't know. In my opinion, maybe Aqba-Hammu wrote and this army is going to him. They said there would be 1,000 men, but this army has only 500.[17]

If the suspicions expressed here were correct, the contingent was on its way to Hammurabi's representative in one of the northern kingdoms, and most likely was to join the Babylonian army assembled there to attack Mari.

The final battles are not documented in our sources, but the conquest seems to have been fast. The records of the final year of Mari's existence do not show any signs of disturbances or panic. The records do suddenly disappear, however, only five months after Zimri-Lim was still sending valuable presents to Hammurabi, and some four months after the defeat of Eshnunna.[18] Hammurabi claimed that he subjugated Mari and its villages as well as many other cities in northern Mesopotamia. The Babylonians occupied the palace of Zimri-Lim (whose fate is unknown) and systematically looted it. It had been known as one of the wealthiest palaces of its days, and its precious objects, statues, and the like were probably carried off to Babylon. Consequently the modern excavators discovered few such objects in the twentieth century. Moreover, Hammurabi's servants carefully went through the archives to remove materials of interest. For example, the letters Hammurabi had sent to Zimri-Lim were almost all removed, as well as the correspondence with Mari's powerful allies, such as Yamkhad and Eshnunna. The rest of the correspondence was packed up and stored in boxes in a central area. Hammurabi's servants attached labels to them and those labels were eventually excavated. They identified the content of the boxes in broad terms and stating when they were packed. For example: "Box with letters of Zimri-Lim's servants, on month 7, day 28 of the year Hammurabi 32."[19] That work was probably facilitated by the fact that Zimri-Lim's archivists had carefully organized the material. Most of the thousands of letters were probably not read beyond the address. What was taken off to Babylon, including letters which must have contained the most important diplomatic correspondence of the Mari kings, is unfortunately now lost to us.

It is unclear how Hammurabi treated the kingdom of Mari after its conquest. No published administrative documents or letters exist from the post-conquest period,[20] so we do not know what took place. It seems, however, that the people of Mari did not submit easily. Two years later, in 1759, Hammurabi had to break their resistance. He claims that he tore down the city walls and turned the land into rubble heaps and ruins.[21] Archaeology shows that his measures were indeed harsh: the entire city was destroyed, including the palace which was burned down. Mari never recovered as a major city, although its name survived and re-appeared in texts, including in a letter from later in Hammurabi's dynasty.[22] A small settlement may have survived on the ruins of the city and most likely a Babylonian administrator represented Hammurabi's interests in the region. Consequently, the king could claim in the prologue of his law code that he showed mercy to Mari's people. In the middle Euphrates region between Babylon and the kingdom of Yamkhad, there was a political vacuum that lasted for several decades.

Although the defeat of Mari was not Hammurabi's final military action, it did complete his project of eliminating his nearby rivals. Larsa and Babylon were unified under his kingship; Eshnunna, Mari and northern Mesopotamia were administered by vassals and officials. The only states in the region where Hammurabi was not fully in control were distant: Elam in the south-east and Yamkhad in the north-west. Smaller states continued to exist to the north of his kingdom, but these posed no threat to him. Hammurabi's supremacy must have been acknowledged throughout Mesopotamia. The introduction to Hammurabi's law code, written after his thirty-eighth year, surveyed the areas he controlled, and boasted of his benevolence toward them. Most attention was paid to the old cities of Babylonia, both in Babylon's and Larsa's former territories. Hammurabi portrayed himself as behaving like a good king. He provided for the people and championed the local gods and their temples. For example, he called himself "the Lord who gives life to the city of Uruk, who guarantees water of abundance to its people, who raises the top of the Eanna temple, and heaps up bounty for the gods An and Ishtar."[23] In the list of places he supported, he included the more distant Malgium, just east of Babylonia, Mari and Tuttul on the middle Euphrates, and the old cities of Assur and Nineveh on the Tigris. Only with respect to Eshnunna did he take a different tone. He favored its gods Tishpak and Ninazu but did not mention the city. Instead, he claimed that he rescued the people from hardship and provided them with peaceful dwellings in the midst of Babylon.[24] This may refer to their deportation to Babylonia.

Years of warfare had fundamentally changed Hammurabi's kingdom. From a small state that competed with its neighbors and was forced to accept the dictates of the distant ruler of Elam, it became the dominant power in the entirety of Mesopotamia.

It is, of course, difficult to assess why Hammurabi undertook these military actions. During the first thirty years of his reign he had participated in the squabbles of the time as a relatively minor player, and only afterwards did he engage in major conquests. The sudden change in attitude in the last decade of his life is never explicitly explained in the sources. It seems likely, however, that Hammurabi's expansionist policy was triggered in the year 1766 by Elam's initial action against Eshnunna and its decision to occupy the territory. The occupation signaled a new policy of the eastern kingdom toward the Mesopotamian states, which was clearly resented. Since Hammurabi's kingdom may have been next on the list of targets, he led the resistance against Elam's expansion. The success in the defeat of the eastern enemy may have inspired Hammurabi to continue the war and establish himself as the dominant force in the region. His actions against Larsa, Eshnunna, and finally Mari followed one another in swift succession, and he may never have disbanded his army. While he was restoring order in Larsa after the conquest of the south (which required more than six months of warfare), he was already moving troops and supplies to Eshnunna. Four months after the defeat of Eshnunna, Hammurabi conquered Mari. His triumphs were thus more the result of one long military action than of a sequence of individually planned campaigns. His successes were certainly due to his army's fighting skills, but he had used diplomacy cleverly as well. Zimri-Lim of Mari, in particular, had been prompted to assist in Hammurabi's conquests, only to be turned against as the final victim. Zimri-Lim may have been convinced to provide forces by the promise that Hammurabi would help him in his aspirations in the north, but in the end Babylon usurped the position of dominant regional power there as well. The creation of his new kingdom may have been the accidental result of a defensive reaction against Elam, but Hammurabi did not scorn the new responsibilities placed upon him. He took it upon himself to guarantee its peace and prosperity, and the final years of his reign show him to have been an able administrator and just king.

7

Governing the New State

By his thirty-third year, after four years of intense military activity, Hammurabi was the ruler of a large territory that incorporated several previously independent states. From the capital at Babylon one could travel 200 kilometers south to the Persian Gulf coast or the same distance north along the Tigris or Euphrates rivers, and still remain in the same kingdom. While the people living in the realm had some common characteristics, there were also many differences and local customs. All had been exposed to Babylonian culture, a thousand-year-old tradition that incorporated elements from speakers of the Sumerian and Akkadian languages. When they wrote, they did so in either of these languages by impressing cuneiform signs on clay tablets. They honored the same pantheon of gods: with very few exceptions, the gods of every part of the state were venerated, although not equally important, everywhere. The people were all aware of cities and how significant they were for life in the region. Although not everyone lived in a city, most people would often see them in the distance, if not visit them.

There were many local peculiarities, however. The inhabitants of cities felt a strong connection to their place of birth. They were first and foremost people of Ur, Larsa, Babylon, etc., rather than inhabitants of a great state. There did not even exist a single name to refer to the entire state. The people's attachment to their hometown was especially visible

in their worship of specific gods. Every city had its own pre-
mier god, whose cult was centered in the main city temple.
The moon god Sin was the leading deity in the southern city
of Ur, the sun god Shamash in the northern city of Sippar, and
so on. These cults dated back to very ancient times, being
often more than a thousand years old, and although all gods
had been merged in a common pantheon as one big family,
the central temple in a city was still primarily devoted to the
original local god. This explains why in the introduction to
his law code Hammurabi mentions city after city, and how he
promoted the local cults: the god Enlil in the city Nippur,
Marduk in Babylon, Erra in Kutha, and so on. He does not
speak of a country under his rule, but of a number of cities,
twenty-five in total, whose patron deities and inhabitants
flourished because of him. Some of these cities were very near
one another and had been under the same political control for
a long time, such as Babylon and Sippar, or Larsa and Ur, but
still the inhabitants saw themselves as first of all belonging to
their hometowns.

The residents of these cities and the surrounding countryside were a varied lot as well. There was a mixture of old
families that had lived in the same place for many generations, and newcomers. The old families could have had roots
going back many centuries, and were heirs to the traditions of
the Sumerians and the Akkadians of the third millennium.
Their culture had become a unified Babylonian one by the
beginning of the second millennium. The newcomers quickly
assimilated the cultures of the cities they came to inhabit,
but still were recognizably different. Many of them originally
did not speak Babylonian, but Amorite. Like Babylonian,
Amorite was a Semitic language, but with a different gram-
matical structure and vocabulary. Originally, it was primarily
spoken by people from Syria, to the north-west of Babylonia.
The native term for Amorite, *amurru*, also meant "the west,"
and could refer to the area of Syria. People from that area
had entered Babylonia over the centuries and many of
them settled in villages and cities. In some places, such as

Mari, the majority of people spoke Amorite, but in the heart-land of Babylonia fewer did so. Everyone used Babylonian for writing, however, and since historians today can only read the written text, they cannot determine what languages the writers spoke.

The sense of a distinct Amorite identity nevertheless survived into Hammurabi's time, despite their presence in Babylonia for at least 250 years. Hammurabi himself regularly referred to his Amorite identity, as did other kings of his and different dynasties. Among his titles, Hammurabi sometimes used "father" or "king of the Amorite land," and part of his name was Amorite (*hammu* meaning "family"). The edict abolishing outstanding debts issued by one of his successors, Ammisaduqa (ruled 1648–1628), distinguished Akkadians and Amorites. It is hard for us, however, to determine who was Amorite and who was not. People's names may reveal what language they spoke at home, but oftentimes Amorite parents gave their children Babylonian names and vice versa.

One indication of Amorite distinctness may have been devotion to the god Amurru, whose name was congruent with the Babylonian term for Amorite. Amurru was a recent addition to the Babylonian pantheon and many people expressed their devotion to him in their names. When someone was called Ibni-Amurru, for example, it suggests that his parents had a special devotion to that god, since the name proclaims that "the god Amurru created him." Similarly, inscriptions on seals indicate a special devotion to that god. Seals were used in Babylonia as a mark of ownership or as the equivalent of a modern signature. When people wrote contracts or witnessed an arrangement, they routinely rolled their seals on the moist clay to verify their action for future consultation. Those seals often had short inscriptions on them to identify the owner, usually with the format: name, son of so-and-so, servant of a god. For example, Tarib-ilim, son of Ina-qati-Shamash, servant of the god Amurru. It is noteworthy in this example that both the seal's owner and his father had good Babylonian names, yet they were devotees of the Amorite god. The forces of acculturation were certainly strong, but it would be mistaken to see all inhabitants in Hammurabi's state to be culturally homogeneous or even speak the same language. Local traditions survived, and a woman of Ur would have seen herself as being different from one of Sippar.

Hammurabi was king of all these diverse people, and he knew well what his role was. He did not change the royal ideology of the time. The king had to be the "good shepherd" of his land, he had to care for his people as if they were a defenseless flock. He had to make them thrive by providing them with food and security. This role also required that he please the gods so that they would shower abundance on the land. Throughout his reign Hammurabi had taken these duties seriously, and he readily adopted the image of the good shepherd. At the start of his law code's introduction he stated "I am the shepherd, selected by Enlil," referring to the god of the Sumerian religious center at Nippur, who headed the pantheon. One of his duties after the war's disruptions had been to make the people safe and prosperous again. In an inscription that was probably written soon after the conquest of the south, Hammurabi portrayed the people of the region (that is, the land of Sumer and Akkad) as scattered sheep whom he had herded back together:

The dispersed people of the land of Sumer and Akkad, I gathered together and I provided pastures and watering places for them. I shepherded them in abundance and plenty and I made them live in peaceful dwellings.[1]

The good ruler provided agricultural wealth for his people, and in southern Mesopotamia where very little rain fell, this meant digging and maintaining irrigation canals to water the fields. The passage just quoted appears in an inscription commemorating such work:

I dug the canal "Hammurabi-is-the-abundance-of-the-people" which brings a profusion of water to the land of Sumer and Akkad.[2]

In three of his year-names Hammurabi boasts of work on canals and many of his preserved inscriptions do as well. During the chronic warfare between the states of the south in the early decades of his reign and before, people upstream had regularly denied water to their southern neighbors by diverting it in river channels that bypassed their cities. Their fields thus became barren. When Hammurabi established control over the region by 1760, he restored the damage and brought water back to areas of the south previously deprived. His unification of the entire south of Mesopotamia, a territory stretching some 400 kilometers from north to south along the Tigris and Euphrates rivers, allowed him to dig long canals connecting various cities. The "Hammurabi-is-the-abundance-of-the-people" canal, for example, ran by Nippur, Isin, Uruk, Larsa, Ur, and Eridu, a distance of some 160 kilometers. Pacification brought thus economic development, and increased the wealth of the population.

The good shepherd also had to maintain order and to protect his herd. The king built city-walls and fortresses and defended the land against foreign invaders. Seven of Hammurabi's year-names commemorate work on walls, either of cities such as Sippar, or at fortified places in the countryside. Late in his reign he claimed to have strengthened walls at Kar-Shamash on the Tigris and at Rapiqum on the Euphrates, most probably the very northernmost borders of his state (the adjacent regions further north accepted Hammurabi's dominance, but were not directly governed by him). A good king also needed to maintain domestic order and Hammurabi did not fail to portray himself as doing so. The introduction to his law code states that the gods had selected him "to make justice come true in the land, to destroy the evil and wicked, so that the strong does not oppress the weak."

These goals could only be accomplished if the gods were kindly disposed toward the land, and an important duty of the king was to guarantee that they were. The Babylonians perceived their gods in very human terms: they had the same needs as people, only on a grander scale. The temples were their houses, in which they were fed, clothed, and groomed by the priests. An elaborate system existed where temple personnel, with the resources provided by vast estates, took care of the gods' needs. The king was responsible for grander projects, since he alone had the resources for large-scale and expensive works. He repaired temple buildings when they were old or damaged, or built new extensions. He paid for fancy thrones, chariots, and cult statues that were decorated with gold, silver, and semi-precious stones. When the gods were pleased, they would provide prosperity to the land in return.

The ideology of the good king connected all of these aspects. The gods chose the king to be the ruler, and in return he took care of their needs and promoted their cults. As a reward, abundance came to the land and the people prospered. The king guaranteed thus that his people were safe and well fed. The surpluses of the land could then be offered to the gods to satisfy their needs. Just like the earlier and later rulers of Babylonia, Hammurabi was careful to portray himself as the central cog in a system that only worked when all parts fit together. Throughout his reign this was the public image he projected in his inscriptions and his year-names.

Letters written by Hammurabi show that this was not mere rhetoric. The king was indeed a conscientious ruler, who wanted the land to prosper and people to receive their fair share. By chance, we still have 180 messages that Hammurabi addressed to officials he had stationed in the south after the defeat of Rim-Sin in 1763. These letters were part of a larger archive that included the correspondence of other administrators, and all were probably sent to one central office in Larsa. The palace in Babylon kept a close watch on the administration of the south. All of these letters date to the last thirteen years of Hammurabi's life, but we cannot place them more accurately in time since letters, unlike contracts and accounts, were almost never dated.

When Hammurabi captured the southern region, its administrative structure was already ages old and centralized in Larsa. He did not need to create an administrative structure anew, but could rely on earlier practices and personnel. Hammurabi did institute some changes, however. First of all, Babylon became the political center, and taxes had to be brought there rather than to Larsa. Secondly, he sent high officials from Babylon and appointed them over the heads of existing officers. He turned the entire kingdom of Larsa into a province called Yamutbal, preserving an old name, and made a Babylonian man, Sin-iddinam, his official representative.

Sin-iddinam, to judge by the letters sent to him, was responsible for a wide variety of palace affairs in the south. He must have had many administrators working under him as specialists in different areas of activity, but among those one is well attested in the letters, one Shamash-hazir. This man was primarily responsible for assigning agricultural fields to palace dependents. He had two titles, "scribe of the fields" and "registrar." His origins are mysterious, but it is possible that he was a member of an old and prestigious family from Larsa, and that his services to the palace remained the same despite the change in political powers. Alternatively, he may have had a long career in Babylon and was sent to Larsa to represent his king there. In a letter found at Mari and addressed to Hammurabi's son Sumuditana, the writer requests that a man called Shamash-hazir return to Babylon, since he had just been appointed palace steward:

I have heard say among my attendants: "Shamash-hazir has become steward. Now that he has been appointed, he has not taken up his post." That is what I heard. Shamash-hazir is with you. Why does he delay a single night now that he has been appointed? Make him leave with my messenger Sakkum, who brought you this letter, and send him to me.[3]

This Shamash-hazir was a personal attendant to the prince, who was promoted to service with the king. He may have moved to Larsa somewhat later. Hammurabi himself advised Sin-iddinam of his arrival. A letter found in Larsa states:

To Sin-iddinam say, thus speaks Hammurabi: Herewith I send you Igmil-Sin, son of Puzur-Shamash, and Nabijatum, the mounted messenger, to receive the fattened animals of Larsa that were under Nabium-malik's control. I also send you Shamash-hazir, the registrar.[4]

Shamash-hazir's function was very important. The king owned enormous estates, especially in the south where he had seized land after the conquest. These needed to be farmed, and this was managed in two ways: portions of the fields were rented out to tenants for an annual fee, while parts were assigned in reward to people who provided other services to the palace. The latter were called sustenance fields. The palace and the royal administration employed a large labor force all over the country, which included specialists in all spheres of activity: priests, craftsmen, soldiers, manual laborers, and so on. Some of the personnel collected rations as payment: daily they received amounts of food (bread and beer) or grain for themselves and their families, and at longer intervals, wool and sesame oil. But the palace preferred another arrangement, which made it less responsible for its workforce on a daily basis. It granted them the use of a field so that they could grow their own food and pay a part of the harvest as rent. Some people were moved from one reward system to the other, as this letter to Shamash-hazir details:

The builder Lipit-Ishtar from Al-Eashar is in the service of the palace, and for a long time has received grain and wool rations. The king has now taken away his grain and wool rations, and has ordered: "Give him a field of 6.5 hectares near his village." I am writing you this order of my Lord, and give him a plot of 6.5 hectares either from his family's fields or from another confiscated field that is available.[5]

Lipit-Ishtar would henceforth be a crown tenant farmer, rather than receive rations from the palace. The system of assigning fields to dependents helped the king in two ways: his land was in productive use without having to pay laborers, and his general labor force was rewarded. The fields assigned to people who provided services often stayed in the same family for generations, since the contract for work done for the palace also passed on from father to son. Not all of the tenants could work the fields themselves, since they were occupied with other duties. They often rented them out to subtenants and thus there was a large number of farmers who worked small plots of land on those estates as well. This system was complicated, but it guaranteed the intense cultivation of all available land, at a time that agricultural income was very substantial.

This arrangement had existed in southern Babylonia for centuries before Hammurabi, and was used by all large landowners, both institutions and private landlords. When Hammurabi conquered the south he continued many of the leases that had been held under Rim-Sin. In a letter concerning one contested field, for example, the official Lu-Ninurta pointed out to Shamash-hazir that "These men have had that field for twenty years already, from before my Lord came down here."[6] It seems that his accountants drew up registers just after the conquest of the south, to determine who worked which fields. Eleven of those are preserved, recording fields in the area of Lagash. They were all written on the 15th and the 16th of the third month in 1761, that is less than eighteen months after Hammurabi conquered the region. For example:

36.54 hectares of agricultural land,
3.42 hectares of low quality land,
(a total of) 39.96 hectares of land with furrows:
Its grain income is 32,875 liters.
The rental payments due were calculated on the basis of the full yield.
1.44 hectares of agricultural land with a grain income of 250 liters,
sustenance plots for individuals at one-half the tax rate,
which the king's oxen plowed.
37.26 hectares of agricultural land,
3.42 hectares of low quality land,
a total of 40.68 hectares of land with furrows:
Its grain income is 33,125 liters;
6 oxen work it;
Ninurta-nasir is the farmer.
Date: Month III, day 16, year Hammurabi 32.
Seal on the tablet: Ninurta-nasir, son of Ilum-shemi, servant of the god Adad.[7]

Hammurabi's officials thus surveyed all existing tenancy agreements in order to determine what rental fees and taxes the palace could expect. They did not change the tenants, however. The difficulty with this method of organization was that it required a great deal of accounting. The plots of land were quite small and consequently there were a great number of them. Registers needed to be kept to indicate who had the right to a field, and that was Shamash-hazir's assignment. Problems arose regularly. Every time someone new started to work for the palace, a field had to be found. Hammurabi's canal projects opened up new tracts of land for cultivation, but often Shamash-hazir had to identify and allocate land in regions where many plots were already occupied. Numerous letters to him deal with this issue. For example:

To Shamash-hazir, Sin-mushallim and their associates say, thus speaks Hammurabi: Herewith I send you the overseer of the coppersmiths, Sin-magir. In his presence insert a stake into the plots that you have demarcated for the coppersmiths, and show the coppersmiths their plots. Send him back then and do not keep him there. Dispatch him soon.[8]

The insertion of a stake was a symbol used to assert someone's right to a field. Shamash-hazir would do this in front of the chief of coppersmiths, who represented his men, and thus the plots were assigned to them. Probably the new tenants kept the stake as proof of the arrangement in the future.

It was a troublesome fact that people sometimes unjustly claimed fields as their own and even started to farm them. Because many of the palace tenants used subtenants to farm their land and had plots in different regions, they could not keep constant watch over all their properties. When they found out that someone else was squatting on it, they had to reclaim their land based on the registers that Shamash-hazir kept, but this was a very complex process. Numerous adjacent small plots were allocated to different people and often they changed hands. A tenant needed to safeguard the document that asserted his rights. Many times people wrote to Hammurabi to complain that their fields had been claimed by someone else, and the king wrote to Shamash-hazir to investigate the matter,[9] or to restore the field to its original tenant and give him grain to make up for the losses he had suffered. These inquiries could prove quite complicated:

To Shamash-hazir say, thus speaks Hammurabi: The shepherd Ili-ippalsam brought the following to my attention: "Four years ago Etel-pi-Marduk took the nineteen hectare field that was assigned to me with a sealed document of my Lord. He continues to take its grain. I have brought this to the attention of Sin-iddinam, but he has not given it back to me." This is what he brought to my attention, and I wrote to Sin-iddinam. If it is true what Ili-ippalsam says, namely that four years ago Etel-pi-Marduk took the nineteen hectare field that was assigned to him with a sealed document of the palace, and that he since then lives off it, then there is no worse thing. Take care of this issue and give Ili-ippalsam back the field according to the sealed document that was drawn up for him in the palace. Also, determine how much grain Etel-pi-Marduk took away from the field over four years by means of the divine weapon, and give it to the shepherd Ili-ippalsam. Send me a report on this matter.[10]

The "divine weapon" mentioned was a standard carried by the royal official, which gave divine authority to the judgments he made. He calculated the income of a field based on the averages of what neighboring plots had produced over the last four years and gave the amount to the wronged shepherd, seemingly taken from the royal storehouse.

Problems of this nature took up most of Shamash-hazir's time. They required him to consult existing records, to establish the rights of people, and to issue compensation for losses. At the same time, he had to satisfy the needs of new personnel and keep records of who received what in new land assignments and compensation. On a regular basis, he had to appear before the king to account for his activities and bring in the registers he had made. In one preserved letter, Hammurabi ordered him to come and report on activities for the last three years:

As soon as you read this letter, collect all the service records you have made, those regarding fields with rental payments, fields of palace attendants, fields of mounted messengers and bowmen, fields of shepherds and shepherd-boys, fields of craftsmen and additional fields, as many as you gave out and assigned, as well as tablets with names and inspections of new service agreements which you have made over the last three years, and tablets regarding palace fields. . . . Bring the surveyors and accountants who work with you, and come to me in Sippar.[11]

Shamash-hazir seems to have been out in the fields interacting with the people, but also in direct contact with the king, receiving numerous letters from him (a total of 83 such letters are preserved). He was not the highest administrator in the region, however, and several of his immediate superiors also wrote to him. The highest official in the province of Yamutbal was Sin-iddinam, whose correspondence is also partly preserved. 112 letters from Hammurabi to him are known, and they discuss a wide array of economic affairs of the palace. All assets of the king's estates were at Hammurabi's disposal and he could order Sin-iddinam to collect and send whatever he wanted. Labor was in great demand, and Hammurabi regularly requested that men with specific skills be sent to Babylon. For example:

As soon as you read this letter, make ready your porters and those of the provincial governors under your authority, who have done work with palace porters before, and place a scribe at their head. He will take travel provisions for one month as rations and one boat with a capacity of 3,000 liters for every ten men. (several lines broken) Not a single one among these porters should be too old or too young. Send me strong men only. They should not be a day later than the date I communicated to you.[12]

Sin-iddinam needed to guarantee that the king's fields would produce income. He was thus responsible for the repair and cleaning of canals and dams. Hammurabi stipulated, for example, "Order that the people who have fields along the

Damanum canal dredge it. The dredging of the Damanum canal should be finished this month."[13] Water management was a complicated business. Sometimes fields that were too far from the head of a canal were located too high to be irrigated, or the water level could be so high that it threatened the crops[14] so that some of it needed to be released into the marshes.[15] Sin-iddinam had to regulate how much water flowed into a canal or a field, and not all farmers were happy with the amount they received. One Sin-gamil, for example, wrote:

I am not getting water from Sin-iddinam for my sesame field. The sesame will die. Don't tell me later: "You did not write to me." The sesame is visibly dying. Ibbi-Ilabrat saw it. That sesame will die, and I have warned you.[16]

Assuming that the fields were successfully harvested, Sin-iddinam had to arrange that the share owed to the palace was shipped to Babylon. He did not collect the income himself, but contracted the work out to merchants. He was responsible for their supervision, however. The king sometimes demanded that the merchants came to Babylon. In this letter to Sin-iddinam, for example, he reiterated his request:

I wrote to you that you should send to Babylon the overseer of the merchants Shep-Sin with 540,000 liters sesame and 9.5 kilograms silver for an old debt, and the overseer of the merchants Sin-mushtal with 540,000 liters sesame and 3.5 kilograms silver for an old debt. You were to collect the wool and send it with them and a section leader. But you answered: "The overseers of the merchants said: 'It is harvest time now. We will go after the harvest.'" They said so, and you reported that to me. Now the harvest has passed. As soon as you read this letter, send them to Babylon, as I wrote before. . . . Let them come and appear before me.[17]

Sometimes cattle and sheep from the palace's extensive herds, as well as wool, were shipped to Babylon. The transport required large ships, which Sin-iddinam either needed to make available[18] or build. In the latter case he had to provide wood and the labor force.[19] As with other palace assets, registrars and overseers kept accounts to document the movement of all these goods and services, and sometimes these men needed to come to the palace in person. In one letter Hammurabi ordered Sin-iddinam to send those who administered the assets of the temples in Larsa:

> As soon as you read this letter, report to all accountants in your province and to Warad-Shamash, son of Eribam and herdsman of the temple of Shamash, that they should come to you with their accounts. Send them to Babylon so that they can make up their accounts here. They should travel day and night so that they arrive in Babylon in two days.[20]

Hammurabi was an impatient man. The trip from Larsa to Babylon was almost 200 kilometers and was hard to cover in forty-eight hours. Repeatedly he made the demand that someone should come immediately, but perhaps his words had little effect. In one letter he had to say:

> I wrote to you that you should send Etel-pi-Marduk. Why did you not send him? As soon as you read this letter, send Etel-pi-Marduk to me. He should not delay, and travel night and day. He should be here soon.[21]

Sin-iddinam represented Hammurabi in non-economic matters in the south as well, assisting the king in legal issues. This regularly involved investigative work to provide evidence and witnesses so that the king could render a legal verdict. Just as Shamash-hazir, Sin-iddinam was typically asked to determine who had the right to a field. He investigated malfeasance. For example, a letter from Hammurabi to Sin-iddinam deals with a case of bribery:

> Shumman-la-ilum told me this: "A case of bribery occurred in Bad-tibira. There are men who took bribes and witnesses who know about it." That is what he told me. I am sending you Shumman-la-ilum with a mounted messenger and a soldier. As soon as you read this tablet, investigate the matter. If there was indeed bribery, put a

seal on the silver and all that was taken as bribes, and send it to me. Also send me the men who took the bribes and the witnesses who know about it, whom Shumman-la-ilum will identify.[22]

Sin-iddinam arrested thieves,[23] investigated the case, and sent the guilty to Hammurabi. The recovery of stolen property was also one of his duties. Such property might include escaped slaves, who found refuge in another town.[24] Sometimes, however, people were enslaved unjustly, as this letter from Hammurabi to Sin-iddinam reveals:

Sin-uselli brought this to my attention: "My son, Sukkukum, disappeared eight years ago and I did not know if he was alive. I made funerary offerings for him as if he were dead. Now I was told that he is living in Ik-bari, in the house of Ibni-Ea, the mounted messenger and goldsmith, son of Silli-Shamash. I went to Ik-bari, but they hid him from me and kept on moving him." This is what he brought to my attention. Now I am sending you a soldier and said Sin-uselli. As soon as they arrive, send a trustworthy man with them. Let them go to Ik-bari and bring back Sukkukum, son of Sin-uselli, and Ibni-Ea who kept him in his house for eight years. Have them brought to Babylon.[25]

One of the major concerns of the king was that he had sufficient men to serve in his army. The troops Hammurabi raised for his conquests numbered 30,000 or more, and most of them came from among the inhabitants of his state. Military duty must have been one of the primary responsibilities of able-bodied men. Since we know neither the total size of the population nor the exact numbers of soldiers who went on campaigns, we cannot estimate how heavy the military burden was. It is clear, however, that Hammurabi wanted to know on how many men he could rely. Immediately after the conquest of Larsa a census of certain professional groups was conducted,[26] most likely to determine who could be enlisted. The management of these affairs was also part of Sin-iddinam's duties. He was routinely asked to provide troops that could be sent anywhere in the state. At one point Hammurabi ordered:

The general who was stationed at Rapiqum (i.e., on the northern border of the state) has left with his troops on a mission. As soon as you read this letter, send one of the generals from your province who has not gone on campaign with troops that are left behind to be stationed in Rapiqum.[27]

Desertion was obviously a crime, yet the confusion after the conquest of Larsa may have encouraged some soldiers to take a chance at it. In another letter, Hammurabi ordered Sin-iddinam:

I have sent (broken name) with men who were stationed at the palace gate but left their post. When they reach you, investigate the matter, take care of their case, and render justice according to the laws that are now in force in Yamutbal. See that proper justice is done.[28]

Sin-iddinam had thus to apply the new laws of Babylon in the province of the south.

Enlisted men provided a service to the king, and like all others who did so, they received the use of agricultural fields as a reward. They were thus in contact with Shamash-hazir, whose job it was to manage these assignments. Soldiers were not given preferential treatment by the king, however, and Shamash-hazir was sometimes reprimanded for taking away land from others and giving it to soldiers:

Sin-ishmeanni from Kutalla, a date-palm gardener informed me: "Shamash-hazir took away the field of my family and gave it to a soldier." That is what he brought to my attention. Is a field under long-term tenancy ever taken away? Take care of this case. If this field is indeed of his family, give it back to Sin-ishmeanni.[29]

Soldiers were a special group of servants, however, and their lives could not have been easy. Beside the fact that they risked death or injury in their normal line of duty, the rewards they received do not seem to have been enormous and were difficult to enjoy. Soldiers had to be available at all times, since they also made up the internal police force of Hammurabi's state. Campaigns were mostly in the summer, which was the time when most labor-intensive agricultural work, especially harvesting, also needed to be done. It was thus often necessary for soldier-farmers to hire someone or make arrangements with someone else to work the fields. There exists a small archive of a soldier who lived in the reign of Hammurabi's second successor, King Abi-eshuh (ruled 1711–1684), which elucidates some of these problems. The soldier's name was Ubarum and he lived in a village to the north of Babylon, Supur-Shubula. These twenty-one tablets illustrate his life at home, not on the battlefield. Ubarum complemented the income of the fields he received from the state with plots rented from others for a share of the harvest. He could not do the farming himself, and had at least two persons with whom he worked. Both caused problems, however. One man who was supposed to work his fields was his brother, but the latter seems to have been uninterested in actually doing any work, perhaps because Ubarum was unwilling to cover his expenses. Thus Ubarum took him to court, an account of which is preserved:

Ubarum spoke as follows before General Sin-ibni: "I sent orders to my brother Ili-sukkal, who lives in the city, to look after my affairs, to plow my fields and to (broken word) the barley, but he refused to plow my field." General Sin-ibni sent for him and they brought him before the court officer. General Sin-ibni and the captains investigated the case. My brother Ili-sukkal said: "I did not say that I would not plow my brother's field or not look after his affairs. He has told a lie to my overseer. Now I declare this. If I do not plow his field on time, I will be responsible. If the field is not plowed by the end of the seventh month, I will measure its harvest out based on the neighboring fields." Ubarum will need to pay the rent for four oxen to his brother Ili-sukkal when he returns from his campaign.[30]

A second solution for the tenant was to engage someone to do the work and divide the income with him. Ubarum hired a man called Ili-iqisham, who was his substitute in the official record. Substitutes were allowed to do work, but not to replace the soldier in actual military duties. Hammurabi's laws were very strict on this score, threatening the death penalty if the soldier was caught. They state:

If a soldier or an auxiliary, who received the order to go on the king's campaign, does not go or hires a replacement and sends him instead, that soldier or auxiliary shall die. The one who denounces him shall take his property.[31]

Unfortunately, Ubarum's arrangements with his substitute did not work well, either. They needed several times go to court to divide the income of the fields between the two, and the substitute's share increased every time. Being unable to do the work himself, Ubarum seems to have had no choice but to agree to each new demand.

The affairs of Ubarum were probably normal for the period, and other soldiers in Hammurabi's day presumably faced similar problems. The king made few provisions to protect them. When a soldier was taken captive by the enemy, his fields were assigned to someone else. The only thing Hammurabi's law code guaranteed was that they would revert to him the moment he returned home (§ 27) or that his son, if old enough, could work them (§ 28). If the children were too young, the wife was given a third of the property so she could secure income to raise them (§ 29). In the event that the captive soldier was found by a Babylonian merchant and was ransomed by him, the laws prescribed a strange sequence of options for the repayment of the merchant. If the soldier had enough assets, he was to pay up himself. If not, first the city-temple's resources were used, and only if those were also insufficient would the palace step in (§ 32). On the other hand, Hammurabi did interfere to facilitate the release of captured men. In a preserved letter addressed to two men, he ordered that funds from a temple be released to ransom someone (it is not clear that the person to be ransomed was a soldier):

To Lushtamar-Zamama and Belanum say, thus speaks Hammurabi: On account of Sin-ana-Damar-lippalis the son of Maninum, whom

Plate 7.1 Photograph of a letter written by Hammurabi to two men in Larsa. He orders them to pay silver to a merchant so that a man captured by the enemy can be ransomed (AbB 9 no. 32) (YBC 4521, courtesy Yale Babylonian Collection)

the enemy has taken, give 10 shekels silver to his merchant from the temple of Sin, and ransom him.[32]

Hammurabi's management style was very direct and the letters indicate that anyone could turn to him when facing a problem. He either rendered a verdict and directed his officials to carry out his orders, or he asked them to investigate the matter further. Nothing seems to have been too trivial for his attention. He asked about small lots of land, single servants, and so on. Some scholars have seen this as a sign that he was a petty ruler, but that is a mistaken judgment. Hammurabi properly fulfilled his functions as king. He was there for his people and all were allowed to approach him. This created a personal bond between the king and his people. They saw that he took care of them, and that he performed his role as a good shepherd. Although we have no single piece of evidence that reveals any popular opinion about him, we can imagine that in his people's eyes he was, indeed, a "good shepherd."

8

Hammurabi,
the Lawgiver

By far the best-known monument connected to King Hammurabi is the black diorite stela engraved with his law code, now on display in the Louvre Museum in Paris. While extremely famous, this monument is also especially enigmatic: historians today are unclear about why it was created and how it was used in antiquity. The modern designation "Code of Hammurabi," analogous to the Code Napoleon of the early nineteenth century, is simple and convenient, but certainly inaccurate. Hammurabi did not codify a new body of laws for his kingdom to guide legal proceedings and inform citizens of their rights and duties. A clear explanation of the purpose of this document is lacking, but a discussion of the contents of Hammurabi's text does provide insights into the legal thinking of his time and the king's use of the monument.

The Louvre stela is engraved with the longest inscription of early Mesopotamian history, about fifty-one columns of text, with between 65 to 106 cases each containing one or a few words. The engraver was clearly very attentive. The cuneiform signs were carefully carved in archaic forms, while the columns were laid out on the front and back of the stela in horizontal bands, also an outdated tradition at the time. In the twelfth century BC, the Elamite king Shutruk-Nahhunte took the Louvre stela to Susa, most likely from Sippar, the city of the god of justice, Shamash. Shutruk-Nahhunte erased some of the columns on the bottom front, probably to prepare the

Plate 8.1   Full view of the stela in the Louvre Museum inscribed with the code of Hammurabi (Réunion des Musées Nationaux/ Art Resource, NY)

surface for an inscription of his own, which was never carved. The monument in Paris was just one of several Hammurabi set up. With it were discovered fragments of at least two other stelae, and probably others had been placed in various Babylonian cities as well.

Although the composition of the text is not explicitly dated, we can estimate that it took place after Hammurabi's thirty-eighth year of rule. The cities and regions mentioned in it as under his control were only then fully conquered. The monument was thus erected in the last years of the king's life, and the text does project a sense of achievement: the king had completed a string of conquests and in celebration he set up this special record.

The inscription has three parts to it: the core is a long list of laws, which are framed by a prologue and an epilogue containing a praise of King Hammurabi in the first person. The prologue, about five columns of text, focuses on his connection to the gods of Babylonia. First Hammurabi explains how they granted him kingship, then he enumerates the gods, their cities, and temples to which he provides support and offerings. For example:

I am the pure prince whose prayers the god Adad knows, who appeases the god Adad, the hero, in the city Karkar, who establishes correct appointees in the Eudgalgal-temple.[1]

In the epilogue, five columns long, Hammurabi focuses on his persona as a just king, one who protects his people, especially the weak among them, from injustice and abuse by the powerful. The first half of the passage reiterates that message in various ways, to be observed both by the people of his own time and by future generations. The second half invokes the gods of Babylonia to curse and punish those who would not heed Hammurabi's pronouncements or change them, especially among the rulers of the future. He wishes upon them death and destruction and the reversal of all good things that gods provide. For example:

May the goddess Nintu, the exalted lady of the lands, the mother who created me, deny him a son and make him not have progeny. May she not generate human offspring among his people.[2]

In between the two parts are listed between 275 and 300 laws (the exact number is unknown because a set of columns was erased in the twelfth century). They are introduced with the statement that Marduk ordered Hammurabi to establish truth and justice, and they are followed by:

These are the just verdicts which Hammurabi the able king has
established. He made the land follow the correct course and proper
conduct.[3]

The laws were all phrased according to the same pattern:
the first part states a potential action introduced by the condi-
tional "if," the second the consequences. The action is most
often a transgression, but not always. An example of a punish-
able offense is "If a man rents a field for farming, but does
not plant grain."[4] A related possible scenario that does not
involve human malfeasance is "If a man rents his field out for
farming and received the rent of the field, and later the god
Adad destroys the field or a flood carries it away."[5] The reper-
cussions are always phrased as commands, for example "that
man shall be killed."

The phrasing of the laws is not guided by principles of
abstraction, seeking to formulate certain rules. In the case of
physical injury, for example, blinding an eye and breaking
a bone are listed separately, instead of expressing the rule
that the same should be done to the perpetrator, whatever
the injury. On the other hand, the elements of individual
cases are removed. While the epilogue states that these are
the just verdicts by King Hammurabi on actual cases, there
are no names of victims and perpetrators preserved. The laws
are thus somewhere between the formulation of rules and
accounts of actual cases judged by the king.

Successive laws regularly refine the conditions of the previous ones, or point out what should happen if a prescribed
punishment cannot be carried out. For example:

If a man neglects to keep strong the embankment wall of his
field and does not strengthen his wall, and a breach opens up in
his wall and the water is allowed to carry away the farmland, the
man in whose wall a breach opened up shall replace the grain that
was lost.[6]

That law is followed by a further statement:

If he is unable to replace the grain, they shall put him and his house up for sale, and the owners of the farmland whose grain the water carried away shall divide (the proceeds).[7]

The Babylonians themselves recognized the coherence of certain groups of laws, although they did not indicate so on the stela in Paris. Somewhat later tablets include a few subject headings, such as "legal verdicts concerning removing property from a house."[8] The full analysis of the organization of the laws is the work of modern scholars, however, and is guided by personal interpretation. This list provides an overview of the subject matters:

paragraphs	*Legal proceedings*
1–5	False witnesses and judges.
	Offenses against property
6–14	Theft of goods, animals, and persons.
15–20	Runaway and stolen slaves.
21–25	Housebreaking and robbery.
	Real estate
26–52	Land tenure.
53–58	Negligent irrigation and unauthorized grazing.
59–65, a	Cultivation of orchards.
b–e, g, h	Arrangements concerning houses.
f, i, j, k	fragmentary
	Financial arrangements
l–cc	Loans and interest rates.
100–112	Mercantile agreements and rules for women innkeepers who give loans.
113–119	Bondage for debt.
120–126	Deposit of goods.
	Women, marriage, family property, and inheritance
127–128	False accusation and marriage.
129–132	Adultery.
133–136	Remarriage of a wife.
137–143	Divorce.

144–149   Concubinage.
150–152   Inheritance and liability for debt.
153   Murder of a husband.
154–158   Incest.
159–161   Financial arrangements at engagement.
162–169   Inheritance.
170–176   Rights of the children of concubines and slaves.
177–184   Property rights of remarried women and priestesses.
185–194   Adoption and substitution of children.

Assault
195–214   Physical injuries, intended and accidental.

Professional fees and responsibilities
215–225   Fees for physicians and veterinarians and penalties for professional mistakes.
226–227   Penalties for removing a slave-mark.
228–240   Fees for builders and boatmen and penalties for professional mistakes.

Agriculture
241–252   Laws concerning oxen.
253–256   Embezzlement.
257–267   Hire of laborers and herdsmen.

Rates of hire
268–277   Rates of hire of animals, wagons, laborers, craftsmen, and boats.

Slaves
278–282   Ownership of slaves.[9]

Many principles underlying these laws can be recognized, and scholars continue to mine the code to investigate the legal thought of the time. A few concepts will be highlighted here as examples.

The most famous rule in Hammurabi's laws is that of "an eye for an eye, a tooth for a tooth," also found in the Hebrew Bible. When someone physically injures another, he will be punished likewise:

If a member of the elite blinds the eye of another member of the elite, they shall blind his eye. If he breaks the bone of another member of the elite, they shall break his bone.[10]

This also applies in cases of negligence:

If a builder builds a house for a man and does not make his work strong, and if the house he built collapses and kills the owner, that builder shall be killed. If it kills the owner's son, the son of the builder shall be killed.[11]

The rule is not that simple, however, as the social statuses of the victim and the perpetrator are taken into account. Only when they are of equal status is the penalty the same as the crime. The list concerning physical injuries continues with:

If he (a member of the elite) blinds the eye of a commoner or breaks the bone of a commoner, he shall pay one pound of silver. If he blinds the eye of a member of the elite's slave or breaks the bone of a member of the elite's slave, he shall pay one-half his price.[12]

On the other hand:

If a member of the elite strikes the cheek of a member of the elite who is of a higher social status than him, he shall be flogged in public with 60 strikes of an ox-whip.[13]

The punishments are thus only equal when the parties involved are socially equal. Otherwise, they can be harsher or more lenient depending on the social differences. The designations of social status in Hammurabi's code are not fully clear to us, however. Three levels are distinguished in Akkadian: *awilum*, *mushkenum*, and *wardum*. We cannot match this with a hierarchy known to us. *Wardum* can be translated as "slave," but the meaning of that term needs to be seen within the Babylonian context. A person indebted to another and unable to repay a loan could become the creditor's slave for a period of time. He was the other's property, and when he was injured his owner was compensated for the loss in value. At times the Akkadian term just meant "servant," however, not a legal dependent, and anyone could declare himself servant of another to show respect. The *awilum* could be a powerful man or one with high status in society, but sometimes the term just meant "man." The *mushkenum* status, literally meaning someone who prostrates, indicated some dependence on another person or an institution, but how that differed from a *wardum* is unclear.

People of a high social class could expect a less severe punishment when they injured a lower ranked person. The eye-for-eye principle was thus not absolute. In general, the penalties Hammurabi lists are very harsh. The death penalty is prescribed some thirty times, including for the theft of temple or palace property (§ 6) or when a run-away slave is given refuge (§ 16). Physical injuries, such as cutting out tongues, eyes or breasts (§§ 192–4) are also common, and public flogging appears as well. There are also some inconsistencies in the punishments that are listed. One law demands the death penalty when something is accepted for safekeeping without a proper document, because the recipient is a thief (§ 7). A related law in another section of the code gives a totally different verdict, however:

If a man gives goods for safekeeping without witnesses or a contract and they deny that he gave it, that case has no basis for a claim.[14]

This type of inconstancy and other elements in the composition of the code strongly indicate that its function was not that of a law book.

The aim of the code remains a much-debated question. From the survey of the laws it is clear that these do not cover all legal affairs that could have arisen. Many areas of activity, often closely related to those discussed, are totally omitted. Whereas cattle and agricultural fields are mentioned, the work of the shepherd is almost entirely ignored. While various possibilities of manslaughter and false accusations of homicide are listed, the straightforward murder of one man by another is not. The laws are mostly very specific and ignore simpler possibilities. Some of the areas of law missing are the organization of justice, the political responsibilities of people, and fiscal obligations to the state. These elements suggest that Hammurabi's inscription is not a law code that seeks to regulate legal principles and judicial procedures in the land. This is not a "Code Napoleon" that tries to impose a uniform system of justice on a newly created state, nor is it a record of the totality of legislation.

Moreover, in the extensive documentation of court cases judged in Hammurabi's reign and afterwards there is no reference to a collection of laws that was the basis for a decision. There is even little agreement between the practical decisions and the rules set forth by the laws. In the large written record from Babylonia in this period there is only one explicit mention of a stela giving information that can be found in Hammurabi's code. In a letter dated in the tenth year of Hammurabi's successor, Samsuiluna, a businessman complained to his deputy about the high costs he incurred. The latter had reported that weavers demanded a daily wage of 15 barleycorns of silver. The businessman replied: "The wages for a hired worker are recorded on the stela,"[15] and told him to pay up until he could come to sort out the matter. Daily wages for weavers were set at 5 barleycorns of silver in Hammurabi's code (§ 271), a third of the demand, but there is no reason to assume that was an absolute rule. Hammurabi could have guaranteed the minimum wage.

In another letter of the period reference is made to a legal principle, without mentioning that it was recorded on a stela. The letter was written by a priestess in Sippar, who complained:

Since my father died, my brothers have not given me the dowry that is stipulated in the contract. Today the matter is clear to me: A priestess whose brothers do not support her in her difficulties, shall give away her inheritance share when it suits her.[16]

The principle she expresses is found on the stela of Hammurabi, in a long law:

If there is an *ugbabtu-*, *naditu-* or *sekretu*-priestess whose father gave her a dowry and recorded it on a tablet, but in that tablet he did not write that she can give her estate to whomever she wishes and does not give her full freedom – after the father dies, her brothers shall take her field and orchard and they shall give her food, oil and clothes corresponding to the value of the inheritance share and they shall keep her comfortable. If her brothers do not give her food, oil and clothes corresponding to the value of the inheritance share and do not keep her comfortable, she shall give her field and orchard to whatever farmer she wants and he shall support her. She shall use the field, orchard, and whatever her father gave her for as along as she lives. She shall not sell it or cover another's expenses with it. Her inheritance share belongs to her brothers.[17]

These few references do not prove, however, that the code was regularly used as a guideline in legal practices of the time, only that certain officially published statements could act as a point of reference in such cases.

The records of court cases indicate that these were judged by groups of men from the communities involved or by the king himself as the highest legal authority. A dispute could be brought to him or to one of these courts and the decisions seem to have been based on common sense. No legal justification, such as reference to a law or to a precedent, was needed. The numerous letters by Hammurabi reveal some of the procedures. Someone who felt that his property had been stolen, for example, could address the king, who had the matter investigated by his officials or considered by groups of judges. The investigation was based on registers and documents, or, if these were missing, on testimonies by witnesses or a divine judge in the form of the river ordeal. Rightful ownership was established and, if needed, the decision was enforced with the help of a soldier. Whatever the verdict, it was not necessary for the judges to explain it by referring to a body of law. That was not the function of Hammurabi's code.

Hammurabi's collection of laws was not the first in Babylonian history. Already 300 years earlier kings issued lists of this type, and these earlier examples elucidate partly how Hammurabi's code was composed. For certain of his laws clear antecedents exist. For example, a nineteenth-century code found in the kingdom of Eshnunna rules:

If an ox is a gorer and the authorities have made this known to its owner, but he does not restrain his ox and it gores someone and thus causes his death, the owner of the ox will pay 2/3 pound of silver.[18]

Hammurabi repeated this as:

If a man's ox is a gorer, and the authorities have made known that it is a gorer, but he (the owner) does not cut off its horns or subdue his ox, and that ox gores and kills a free man, he (the owner) will give half a pound of silver.[19]

When Hammurabi's code was written, the authors thus based themselves partly on these older texts. Since Hammurabi's code was longer, however, they needed to formulate new cases, and probably used various means to do so. If there was already a law about injury to an eye, for example, it was very easy to write another one about a bone, using simple parallelism. It seems also that actual verdicts by the king lay at the basis of new clauses. This best example of such practice derives from a letter written by Hammurabi's old rival Rim-Sin of Larsa, where he states: "You throw the slave into a kiln, because he threw a boy into the oven."[20] Such a decision could easily have led to a law such as, "If a slave throws a boy into the oven, they shall throw him into a kiln." As Hammurabi judged many cases, there was an abundance of opportunities to formulate new laws based on them. The first sentence of the epilogue, which states that the preceding cases were just verdicts by the king, advises the reader that these were at the basis of the laws.

That does not make a legal code, however, and the question remains what the purpose of this monument was. Hammurabi's text itself provides the answer. In the epilogue the king explains the intended use of the stela. He had two audiences in mind: the people of his own time and future kings. About the first group Hammurabi states:

Let a wronged man who has a court case come to the statue of me as King of Justice and let the words of my stela be read out to him. Let him hear my precious words. Let my stela make his court case clear to him. Let him see his verdict, and set his mind at ease saying: "Hammurabi . . . brought about well-being for the people forever and made the land have just ways."[21]

Someone who felt wronged could thus find solace in the monument, because it showed that justice would prevail in the end. Hammurabi guaranteed that his country was correctly ruled. He protected the weak from abuse by the powerful, he sheltered the widow and the waif, and his stela announced that to all.

The second audience of the stela which was explicitly acknowledged was the future king. To him, Hammurabi says: "Forever in the future may a king who rules this land see the words of justice I wrote on my stela." He is not to change or remove them, but use them as a guide for his own rule:

May he guide his people correctly. May he judge their cases and give decisions. May he remove the evil and the wicked from his land. May he make his people happy.[22]

Hammurabi was the King of Justice, a title he uses repeatedly in his epilogue. He was the shining example in this respect for all future generations, and he proclaimed his own grandeur by means of his stela. That is why several copies of the stela were most likely erected in various cities. This was just one aspect of several that the king celebrated in his public monuments. The exemplars of the law code were among many the inscribed stone monuments dedicated to Hammurabi that were set up during his reign. Other inscriptions on stone were found in such cities as Ur, Kish, and Sippar. Those are unfortunately only known from fragments, but their general content is still recognizable. In them Hammurabi is praised as a warrior whose conquests brought peace and prosperity to the world. Such monuments could only be distributed throughout Babylonia after Hammurabi had conquered the territory, and they are a tribute to his military skills. Similarly the law code acknowledges his conquests, but its focus was on the correct way in which Hammurabi ruled the land. As a good king he guaranteed that all people were judged fairly and did not have to fear abuse of power. This message coincided with actual practice that we can observe in Hammurabi's letters to his officials. Anyone who felt wronged could turn to him for a verdict. The monumental stela in the Louvre, and others now lost, remained visible testimonies to Hammurabi's greatness as a just king after his death. For centuries scribes copied out the text on clay tablets, which were created until the fifth century BC. The text of Hammurabi's code became an ancient document with special status. These copies engendered the dominant element of Hammurabi's legacy, one that is still with us today: he was the paradigm of a just king.

9

Hammurabi's Character

What kind of man was Hammurabi? While we do have a substantial amount of information on his actions, we still are greatly at a loss when trying to determine aspects of his personality and personal life. He was a powerful ruler and, like all his colleagues, he was head of a large family, probably with several wives. It was the habit of the time that a conqueror would take over the women attached to the palace of the king he defeated, and most likely Hammurabi did so as well. None of these women is known by name, however. Probably he had numerous children, but the sources are not explicit on those either, and we know the names of three sons only. Before the sack of Mari in 1761, one Sumuditana, guest of Zimri-Lim, appears as the oldest son and thus the crown-prince. He must have died before his father, however, or have fallen into disgrace, as another son, Samsuiluna, was Hammurabi's successor. Mari was also visited by a younger son, Mutu-numaha, about whom we know nothing more.

All of the documented interactions of Hammurabi relate to his role as king: he led his armies, engaged in international relations and governed his state. From the numerous letters that discuss these issues, especially from the Mari archives, we can obtain some sense of how Hammurabi interacted with others and of his character. Letters regularly present direct quotes of the people involved in a conversation. They were not dictated, however, and were reconstructed by the sender of the letter who put his own spin on the words. Moreover, the scribes who actually wrote out the tablets could change the wording and paraphrase to a certain extent. So the quotes we read may have been substantially changed from what was said. Hammurabi himself was the author of a few letters that were found in Mari, and there are a good number of missives to his officials. The latter often sound similar in tone, and likely represent standard phrases rather than the king's actual words. Thus they are not very informative in this respect.

Yet, some of the Mari letters written by Zimri-Lim's representatives in Babylon relate the discussions Hammurabi held with others and give a sense of his behavior, his interests and concerns. One such report was written to Zimri-Lim by Ibal-pi-El, who had good access to Hammurabi. He sent it during the preparations for the war against Elam, around the year 1765. The letter describes several days of interactions between the Mari envoys and Hammurabi:

To my Lord say, thus speaks Ibal-pi-El, your servant: I spoke to Hammurabi about the return of the Khanean tribesmen, and two days before the arrival of Yaqqim-Addu I sent them back to my Lord. Two days after the departure of the tribesmen, Yaqqim-Addu arrived, and we discussed the organization of a celebration by the tribesmen for which Yaqqim-Addu had come. Since the tribesmen had left, we covered up the matter.

But, we put to Hammurabi all the matters with which my Lord charged Yaqqim-Addu. Two days after Yaqqim-Addu had completed his mission, we went back to Hammurabi and Yaqqim-Addu asked for orders. He answered: "I want to let you go. Go!" This is what Hammurabi told him.

We answered him as follows: "Will you, Lord, send back Yaqqim Addu without any troops? This is what you keep on writing to our Lord: 'Go up to the land of Subartu and turn the kings there to our side.' That you keep on writing to our Lord. Now, you are not sending any troops to our Lord? How could our Lord go up to the land of Subartu without many troops?" That is what we answered him.

He said: "At the end of this month the enemy will consult the omens, to which the god will give no reply. He will meet his undoing, a good thing. Let Yaqqim-Addu stay here another five days until we see the full plans of the enemy. Let us get the full plans of the enemy, so that I can give him detailed instructions and he can go." That is what he said.

After this tablet of mine, Yaqqim-Addu will gather complete information and come to my Lord. 60 soldiers of my Lord and 60 Babylonians went to the gate of Mankisum and captured an informant. They took the informant to Lord Hammurabi, so that he can interrogate them. My Lord's army is well.[1]

The long account first acknowledges the fact that Hammurabi had agreed to send soldiers belonging to the Khanean tribesmen back to Zimri-Lim, something that he was often reluctant to do. At the height of his wars, Zimri-Lim regularly requested that his men be sent home, but Hammurabi often delayed. He still badly needed Zimri-Lim's support against Elam at this time, however, which may explain his attitude. But their return was not the purpose of Yaqqim-Addu's visit to Babylon. He wanted Hammurabi to send Babylonian troops to Zimri-Lim, so that the king of Mari could bolster his position with the rulers of the north and force them to switch allegiance to the Babylon–Mari coalition.

Hammurabi was unwilling to give up men for such matters, an attitude that appears in many letters. Repeatedly Zimri-Lim asked for soldiers and he was rebuffed with various excuses. For example, a later letter from Ibal-pi-El to Zimri-Lim quotes Hammurabi as saying:

Why do you want to change the things that we agreed on: "When I send you a group of 100 men, people will hear about it and speak as if it were 1,000 men. If I should send you 1,000, they would speak of it as 10,000. The very day that the enemy would hear of it, he would be very worried." In five days we will have full information. Then we will consider things and act according to what we have learned. I will not send any troops before we have full information on the situation.[2]

There are many other occasions where Hammurabi rejected similar requests for help by Zimri-Lim. Usually he asked for more time in order to assess the situation, as he did in the interactions with Ibal-pi-El: "Let Yaqqim-Addu stay here another five days until we see the full plans of the enemy." Hammurabi justified the delay by stating that the enemy would take oracles later in the month, and that these would reveal the gods' displeasure. Hammurabi's belief in oracles was normal for the time. Everyone thought that the gods did communicate messages about the future through various signs: events of nature, such as strange births; astronomical occurrences; dreams; and numerous other phenomena. It was the duty of professional diviners to observe these signs, and they could also take special actions to inquire what the gods had in mind. Among those actions it was very common to cut open a sheep and examine its liver. The colors and shapes of certain parts would provide answers about whether the future would be auspicious or not. Sometimes several diviners undertook the examination jointly. A letter found at Mari relates how diviners from that city collaborated with those of Hammurabi:

When we do the divination, a diviner of Hammurabi does an analysis together with me. With Inib-Shamash a second diviner does a second analysis. Then we compare our analyses.[3]

Yearly thousands of sheep were sacrificed for this purpose. The advice of diviners was important for all matters of state and military actions. Kings would ask them to provide answers to specific questions. When Hammurabi put pressure on Zimri-Lim to yield the city of Hit, the latter asked his diviner for guidance on whether or not to give in:

Take emergency oracles about the yielding of Hit to the king of Babylon. Ask: "Should Zimri-Lim yield Hit to the king of Babylon? Would he be safe? Would his country be well and flourish?"

The diviner replied:

I have used two lambs as follows. I asked: "If Zimri-Lim gave Hit to the king of Babylon, would he be safe and his land in good condition, and would it expand?" The omens I obtained were unfavorable.

Then I took the oracles asking: "If Zimri-Lim did not give Hit to the king of Babylon, would he be safe and his land in good condition, and would it expand?" I took these oracles so that you would not yield. The omens I obtained were favorable.

My Lord should refuse Hit and its territory to the king of Babylon and not yield them.[4]

Hammurabi himself used diviners regularly, for example before attacking Larsa.[5] Because of their importance in the decision-making process, the status of diviners in the courts was very high. They were members of the king's secret council and took part in the most important policy discussions. Consequently, they could secure other responsibilities, such as leading armies and governing provinces. This explains how the diviner Aqba-Hammu could become ruler of Qattara after Hammurabi gained control over that city (see chapter 5).

It is remarkable that in his interactions with Ibal-pi-El Hammurabi was so confident that the enemy would be in trouble and be destroyed. Elam had not yet consulted the oracles, so the outcome was unknown to everyone. Perhaps Hammurabi had done his own consultations and had received a reassuring message from the gods. In any case, he remained cautious and asked Yaqqim-Addu to stay another five days so that the enemy's intentions would become clear. Hammurabi requested five extra days almost every time he was confronted with an urgent demand; he replied then that he needed the time to get more information. During the siege of Larsa, for example, he repeatedly countered Zimri-Lim's desire to get troops with explanations like this:

I will want another five days. If in five days I have taken Larsa, I will send a heavily equipped army to Zimri-Lim, but if I have not taken the city in five days, I will take whatever I can out of the army and send it to him.[6]

The five-day period seems to have been a standard unit of time and other people employed the concept as well. It gave respite from immediate demands and Hammurabi seems to have preferred that to making up his mind quickly. This is in stark contrast with his own demands on his officials and the time he gave them to obey his orders. The letters he sent to Larsa constantly stated that people had to appear in Babylon in two days, a 200-kilometer long journey that normally took more time. Naturally, these are rhetorical expressions, but the consistent use of two days when he ordered something and five days when he needed to fulfill a request does show that Hammurabi was more eager to receive than to give.

Ibal-pi-El's report to Zimri-Lim depicts Hammurabi as behaving diplomatically, although he politely resisted the requests of an important ally. Hammurabi treated Zimri-Lim's envoys with respect, although he refused to budge on sending troops. He was not always that polite, however, even with Zimri-Lim's men. A slightly later letter from La'um to Zimri-Lim reports an outburst by Hammurabi in a situation where diplomatic protocol had been breached.

To my Lord say, thus speaks La'um, your servant: We went in to have a meal with Hammurabi and entered the palace courtyard. Zimri-Addu, Yarim-Addu and I, we three only were given a robe, while all the people of Yamkhad who came with us were given a robe. Since he had dressed all the people of Yamkhad, while he did not dress the secretaries that serve my Lord, I said to Sin-bel-aplim (Hammurabi's minister of foreign affairs) on their behalf: "Why do you separate us as if we were sons of pigs? Whose servants and secretaries are we? We are all servants of a king of the first rank. Why do you create enmity between right and left?

This is what I said to Sin-bel-aplim. I had an argument with Sin-bel-aplim and the secretaries of my Lord became angry and left the courtyard. They related this matter to Hammurabi and they gave them all robes. Once they were dressed, Tab-eli-matim and Sin-bel-aplim reproached me and said this: "This is what Hammurabi tells you: 'From the break of dawn you don't stop annoying me. Are you in charge to decide about garments in my palace? I dress whomever I like and don't dress whomever I dislike. I will never again dress simple messengers at the occasion of a meal.'" My Lord should know that this is what Hammurabi said.[7]

Hammurabi had thus a sharp edge and could lose his temper, albeit not directly to the party involved here. When his relations with Zimri-Lim deteriorated, he did explode, however, as was reported to the Mari king:

> When Hammurabi opened his council meeting, he could not stop crying and repeatedly invoked god to hate my Lord. And this is what he said: "It would be unlikely if in two months I did not take revenge on him and make him kneel down in the dust! Envoys from Elam have come to offer peace and I am tempted to say yes." At the moment Elamite envoys keep on coming to Babylon and they don't even stay for a single day as one replaces the other. I also hear around me: "Since he has seized the hem of the robe of Eshnunna's ruler, I want to make him pay for it." My Lord should know this.[8]

This happened a few months before Hammurabi marched on Mari and captured it. The conquest did not lead to an immediate destruction of the city, however. That took place two years later, probably in response to a rebellion, when Hammurabi reduced the palace to a ruin and turned Mari into a minor village.

Hammurabi's ruthless vengeance for disobedience is also attested in other situations. As would be expected, he did not accept treason and he severely punished people who conspired with the enemy. Such an event took place in the war with Elam, as was reported to Zimri-Lim:

> To my Lord say, thus speaks Yarim-Addu, your servant: Among the Babylonian troops that were captured (by the Elamites) last month was a section-leader from Mutiabal who said this to the ruler of Elam: "The entirety of Mutiabal has waited for this moment. Send me back to my country so that I can make it rebel in your favor." This is what the man said to the ruler of Elam, and he sent him back to Babylon. He arrived in Babylon and saw the king, but did not reveal his intent. Then he left for Kazallu, and this man conveyed the message of the ruler of Elam. The people of Kazallu took note, made up their minds, and wrote to the ruler of Elam.
>
> This affair became known to Hammurabi and he acted shrewdly. He sent spies who assessed the situation. When they confirmed that

the whole thing was true, he addressed the leaders of Kazallu as follows: "Because of the Elamite threat, all the people should gather grain and straw and bring it all to Babylon . . . so that your country will not be looted. . . . Gather grain and straw, and boys and girls and bring them all to Babylon. . . . You can continue to graze your sheep in your country, and you can continue to live in your houses." This is what the king told them and they answered: "Because our Lord said so, we will do it. Let us make arrangements." This is what they answered the king and they left. After they left, Hammurabi sent 6,000 men with boats to ship their grain and transport their families. They tried to find excuses(?) and said: "We have not yet made arrangements. Stay with us." This they said to the men the king had sent.

On the third day, they received a message from the ruler of Elam. Relying on his protection, they rebelled as one against Hammurabi and killed as many of his men as possible. Hammurabi heard the news of their uprising and sent troops to that country. The entire army of Mutiabal gathered to confront and fight him, but he routed them. He deported them all, men, women and children.[9]

The land of Mutiabal, located around the city Kazallu only some twenty kilometers north-west of Babylon, intended thus to rebel against Hammurabi with the support of Elam. Hammurabi tried to trick the people: he offered to safeguard their harvest and children against an Elamite raid, with the intent, in reality, of holding them hostage. The people of Mutiabal saw through this plan and delayed handing over their property until they heard from the ruler of Elam that he would help. Hammurabi acted immediately, however, and they failed to counter his invasion. He showed no mercy and deported the entire population to Babylon. According to another Mari letter he also "destroyed their houses and burned them down."[10] Deportations were far from unusual in this period, and Hammurabi regularly brought people from conquered territories into Babylonia. It is unlikely that he was more ruthless than his contemporaries, and after all a rebellion so close to home could not be tolerated. But the episode shows that he could act very decisively and promptly.

The diplomats who dealt with him were well aware of his importance and at times humiliated themselves or their

Plate 9.1 Head of an aged man excavated at Susa. Although there is no inscription, the head is often thought to represent Hammurabi (Réunion des Musées Nationaux/Art Resource, NY)

masters to gain his favor. When Ishme-Dagan's envoys came to Hammurabi to plead for support against attacks from high-landers, they described their king as a doormat under his feet.[11] At the end of his life, no one equaled Hammurabi in power, and proper respect was his due.

We do not know much about Hammurabi's later years. The last year-name that mentions military action was his thirty-ninth, which states that he slaughtered people from the north. By then, the king must have been in his fifties, if not older, a considerable age at that time. Naturally, someone else could have led the campaign. Hammurabi lived four more years, ruling for a total of forty-three. One letter written by his successor, Samsuiluna, suggests that he was ill and handed over the rule of the land to his son before his death. But, unfortunately, that passage in the text is damaged, so we are not certain whether this was the case. In 1750, the throne of Babylon certainly passed on to a new king, who, for about a decade, enjoyed the stability that his father had created. But then Hammurabi's state started to deteriorate fast; the kingdom had truly been his own.

10

Hammurabi's Legacy

The code of Hammurabi remains an eloquent and powerful statement: the king was a man of justice, the shining example of a just ruler to be remembered for eternity. This peaceful image dominates the text, but it was not the only one that Hammurabi's court wanted to convey in this and other official statements. The code makes clear that he could dispense justice only because he had conquered – or in his words pacified – the world. It portrays thus an age-old belligerent ideology that military action is a justified means to bring peace and justice to the conquered lands. In other writings about Hammurabi, his courtiers emphasized the martial aspects of his rule, but they remained attached to the justification that these actions were for the cause of justice and peace. The king's accomplishments were considered exceptional by his contemporaries, and the honors his courtiers bestowed on him surpassed those allotted to other kings of his dynasty. The image they had of him was multifaceted, albeit always fully positive. Later generations in Mesopotamia were inspired by the exalted portrayal that existed at the end of his reign, and looked back at him in a special light as well, and that tradition has also inspired modern scholarship. A careful reading of the sources can round out the personality of Hammurabi in more complex ways, however.

The list of laws in Hammurabi's code ends with the statement that these were the just decisions made by the king.

They demonstrate how he was a just ruler, and the epilogue explains what that meant: He cared for his people over whom the god Marduk had appointed him shepherd, he brought peace and light to them. The text goes on to explain how he was able to do so:

With the powerful weapon that Zababa and Ishtar granted me, the insight Ea decreed for me, and the ability Marduk gave me, I wiped out the enemies everywhere.[1]

Warfare had thus been important, but it was not endless nor an end in itself. The epilogue continues to state, "I put an end to battles," and "I am the shepherd who brings peace."[2] The idea of peace and protection that Hammurabi provided dominates the epilogue, but there is also a clear acknowledgment that it was only accomplished through military means. Looking at the prologue with that idea in mind, we understand that the statements there do not only provide a list of cities on whom Hammurabi bestowed abundance; the king indicates that these are his conquests.

Almost the entire prologue is taken up with a survey of twenty-five cities whose deities and temples received special attention from the king. They are organized in four groups. The first lists the seven major cult centers in Babylonia: Nippur, Eridu, Babylon, Ur, Sippar, Larsa, and Uruk. Southern and northern Babylonian cities are joined together through the family relationships of their patron deities. Enlil, the old and venerable Sumerian god of Nippur, was still considered the head of the pantheon. His brother Ea of Eridu, was the father of Marduk, the god of Babylon. The sun god Shamash was patron deity both of Sippar in the north and Larsa in the south, so the two cities appeared side-by-side. The gods Sin and Anu were also among the most prominent in the pantheon, and their cities, Ur and Uruk, in the south were important ancient centers. Only through the annexation of the south had Hammurabi been able to bring those city-gods together in one list. He had gathered the main gods of the Babylonian pantheon in one land.

The prologue continues to explain Hammurabi's relations with three groups of cities whose gods did not belong to the highest pantheon, organized on a geographical basis. First were the cities in the center of the country, close to Babylon: Isin, Kish, Kutha, Borsippa, Dilbat, and Kesh, going in a circle around the capital. Then the text lists cities in the east of Babylonia, moving from south to north: the twin cities Girsu and Lagash, Zabalam, Karkar, Adab, and Mashkan-shapir. Finally, cities to the north of Babylon are enumerated: Mari and Tuttul, which are artificially presented as twin cities, Eshnunna, Akkad, Assur, and Nineveh. The last two groups had only recently been subdued. While those of the east had been annexed to Hammurabi's state, those of the north had been defeated but remained outside Babylonia. The focus of Hammurabi's relationship with these cities was on his charitable works, but it was clear to all who heard the list that he had acquired most of them through military action. When he mentions the cities of Larsa and Mari, conquered after long wars, he stresses how he showed mercy to their peoples.

Because of his conquests, Hammurabi had been able to bring justice to the entire world surrounding him and this peaceful theme remains by far the strongest of the stela's text. That principle was not only communicated in written form on the stela. The relief on the top was also understandable to nonliterate people – that is most of the population – and it showed how the sun god Shamash, the protector of justice, gave a rod and a ring – probably the emblems of justice – to Hammurabi. That message was thus the most accessible to the majority of the population, and the clearest. The military conquests were secondary.

Hammurabi's military prowess was not always downplayed, however. In a number of literary compositions about him, the authors focused on the fact that he had defeated enemies all over the world. They praised the king as a warrior, using a vivid imagery of powerful forces from nature and battle. These hymns were routinely carved on stone stelae that Hammurabi set up in several cities, both in the north (Kish, Sippar) and in the south (Ur) of his country. Many of those contained the inscription repeated in the two written languages of the kingdom, Sumerian and Akkadian. They are now most often in a very fragmentary state, and we do not know when the stelae were broken. The pieces had been kept together, however, which shows that the inscriptions were considered to be especially important. The incomplete condition makes it difficult to comprehend the structure of these texts, but we can discern the main messages. Conquest and power play a prominent role in the way Hammurabi is described in them. In a stela, possibly excavated at Sippar, it is stated:

Hammurabi, king, mighty warrior, exterminator of enemies, flood of battles, destroyer of enemy lands, who puts an end to wars, who resolves disputes, who destroys soldiers like figurines of clay.[3]

Plate 10.1 Fragment of a statue inscribed with a hymn in praise of Hammurabi (King 1898 no. 60; from C. J. Ball, *Light from the East*, London, 1899, 69)

A stela excavated at Ur contains a similar message:

> I am the hero among heroes, the furious one among the proud, perfect in youth and heroism. I beat down with my mighty weapon the land that does not submit to Marduk.[4]

These actions were not purely destructive, however. Also in these passages it is clear that Hammurabi fought to end war and discord. The enemies he destroyed had brought chaos, and their removal eradicated the problems that confronted the land. His mission was not limited to Babylonia, but extended to the entire world. Another fragment of the Ur stela states:

> The people of Elam, Gutium, Subartu, and Tukrish, whose mountains are distant and whose languages are obscure, I placed into his hand. I myself continued to put straight their confused minds.[5]

The distant mountain lands to the east and north of Babylonia, whose defeats were also mentioned in Hammurabi's year-names, were very different from his land. People there were so confused that they spoke in incomprehensible tongues, but Hammurabi brought order to them. He subjected them to the control of a Babylonian god (whose name is lost). His conquests were thus not to increase Hammurabi's power and possessions, but they had a civilizing mission. The world benefited from the fact that he conquered it.

The inscription on the Ur stela was partly copied out on a tablet and inserted in a longer hymn in which Hammurabi praised himself. It contains a long list of attributes of the king, who portrays himself as a powerful force that conquers evil and disrespect for the god Marduk. For example:

> I am the king, the brace that grasps wrongdoers, that
>   makes people of one mind,
> I am the great dragon among kings, who throws their
>   counsel in disarray,
> I am the net that is stretched over the enemy,

I am the fear-inspiring, who, when lifting his fierce eyes,
   gives the disobedient the death sentence,
I am the great net that covers evil intent,
I am the young lion, who breaks necks and scepters,
I am the battle net that catches him who offends me.[6]

The motif that dominates the law code also found its way
into these praises of Hammurabi's military achievements.
It is such an integral feature of his fame that it is never forgotten.
After glorifying Hammurabi's valor in battle, the hymn
on the clay tablet clearly proclaims his dominant attribute
with the statement:

I am Hammurabi, the king of justice.[7]

The stela from Ur also contains this passage:

(I am) the just, the righteous man. Because it is foremost, the word
that I speak is not to be dismissed. May they praise my ability and
his greatness.[8]

Three concepts were thus constantly joined in the portrayal
of Hammurabi: he was powerful in battle, he brought peace,
and he brought justice. Each hymn or inscription may have
focused on one of the three, but all aspects had to be linked to
give full honor to the king.

Hammurabi was not the only king of the early second
millennium who was revered in these ways. His courtiers
utilized a store of images and epithets that had been in use
for centuries. He did receive more elaborate honors, however,
and he was praised in ways that were unusual for kings of
his dynasty. Perhaps the highest esteem awarded him was
his inclusion among the gods during his lifetime. He is called
the god Hammurabi, the good shepherd, in one song that celebrates
how the gods of the south respect him.[9] At the same
time people named their children after Hammurabi. The name
Hammurabi-ili, meaning "Hammurabi is my god," appeared,
something unparalleled in his dynasty. The references to

Hammurabi as god were probably inspired by a southern tradition, where regularly kings were deified during their lifetime. This had happened to Rim-Sin whom Hammurabi had replaced. Upon his death, Hammurabi's status was thus very special. Naturally the fact that he had ruled the country for forty-two years was important; many people had never known another king. But, his accomplishments had indeed been unusual and deserved special praise.

It is thus no surprise that later generations remembered him more than any other king of the early second millennium. Over time, his prominence increased, and he became one of the few kings of the ancient past to whom people referred more than a thousand years after his death. This fame became increasingly focused on his non-military achievements. It was not Hammurabi the conqueror who was honored, but the king as lawgiver. Because of his prominence in the area of law he was so well known to later generations that he became a point of reference for anything related to his distant past. About a century after his death an Akkadian poem in honor of Ishtar as the goddess of war, states explicitly that it was originally composed for Hammurabi:

The king who (first) heard this song as a sign of your heroism is Hammurabi. This song for you was composed in his reign. May he be given life forever![10]

Although not explicitly dated, the grammar and style suggest that the poem was composed in the reign of Ammisaduqa of Babylon, Hammurabi's fourth successor. The reference to the earlier king gave the song more prestige. Poems of this type were composed and copied in schools, and a connection between Hammurabi and that institution had existed in his own days as well. A fragmentary hymn of his reign stated, "In the school the praise of your kingship is in everyone's mouth."[11]

Hammurabi appears in the later literature of his dynasty in a very different context; an ironic dialogue between a woman and her unfaithful lover. Whereas she declares true love for

him, he rejects her as rudely as possible. In one of his statements, he invokes the goddess of love and Hammurabi:

> I swear to you by Nanaya and king Hammurabi,
> I am telling you my real feelings,
> Your love is nothing more to me than worry and grief.[12]

It is a sad use of an oath before god and king to give his
rejection more strength.

The physically most striking reminder of Hammurabi was
the stela inscribed with his laws. During the reigns of his
immediate successors, students and others copied out parts of
the text on clay tablets, sometimes introducing some interpretation. Three manuscripts made under later kings of his
dynasty inserted, at irregular intervals, subject headings
before groups of laws, such as, "legal decisions concerning
contracts of hire and purchase."[13] Another type of study
involved the translation of part of the text into Sumerian. A
tablet from Sippar contains a translation of the curses in the
last column of the code as it appears in the stela from the
same city.[14] This shows how scribes studied the text to bring
order to it, and used it as basis for their scholarly work.

The memory of Hammurabi's achievements did not disappear with the end of his dynasty some 150 years after his
death. Although the political situation in Babylonia changed
drastically, the stelae with his code remained in place. This
was not unusual: stone monuments of other rulers, including
some who had lived 500 years before Hammurabi, stayed on
view as well. So when, in the year 1158, the Elamite king
Shutruk-Nahhunte I raided Babylonia, he carted off a large
number of stone monuments to his capital Susa, including
Hammurabi's complete stela from Sippar and two others, possibly already broken at the time. His loot also included such
famous works of early Babylonian art as the stela of Naram-
Sin and the obelisk of Manishtushu. King Shutruk-Nahhunte
had the original inscriptions on most of these monuments
erased and replaced them with texts commemorating his raid.

On Hammurabi's stela four or five columns were wiped out, but a new inscription never was engraved.

By the time the stela had disappeared from Babylonia, copies on tablets must have been distributed throughout scribal schools, and these were used as the basis of later manuscripts. Scribes all over Mesopotamia continued to produce more copies for centuries. Manuscripts from all cities with major scribal schools are preserved, and several copies were kept at the seventh-century Assyrian library of Assurbanipal. A catalogue from that library includes "The Laws of Hammurabi" among its holdings.[15] Scholars of the first millennium wrote interpretations of the laws, but these are unfortunately very poorly preserved. The latest copy of a part of Hammurabi's code known to us was found in a fifth-century library in the sun god's temple at Sippar, near the famous stela's original location.

This preservation of Hammurabi's memory placed him in a special league with only a handful of other kings. He became a ruler of the past to whom one could refer as a famous ancestor or as a fixed point in time that people would recognize. Hammurabi had died in 1750, but one thousand years later rulers of the land of Suhu, the area along the Euphrates just to the north-west of Babylonia, referred to him as a distant ancestor. One Shamash-resha-usur stated that he was a direct descendant of Hammurabi, five generations removed. His son, Ninurta-kudurri-usur, claimed to be the "distant descendant of Tunamissah, son of Hammurabi, king of Babylon."[16] Tunamissah is otherwise unknown, but his name suggests that he belonged to the group of people that ruled Babylonia after Hammurabi's dynasty, the Kassites. Tracing the lineage back to Hammurabi made sense for a ruler of the Middle Euphrates region, since that king had indeed controlled it in the very distant past. Hammurabi's authority was also invoked by Ninurta-kudurri-usur when he declared that he re-established the offerings of the god Adad "according to the commands of Hammurabi, king of Babylon,"[17] once identified as "a king who preceded me."[18] These men attempted to give themselves a more exalted status by claiming that they descended from Hammurabi, but did not know how long ago he lived. Therefore they merely stated that it was many generations ago.

Around the year 550, the last independent Babylonian king, Nabonidus, tried to attach a number of years to how long before him Hammurabi had reigned. In inscriptions commemorating the restoration of the very ancient temple of the sun god Shamash in Larsa, he claimed that he had found the original building inscription by Hammurabi:

> An inscription with the name of Hammurabi, an ancient king, who 700 years before Burnaburiash built the Ebabbar and the temple-tower for the god Shamash on top of old foundations.[19]

Nabonidus' calculations were substantially off: King Burnaburiash ruled in the mid-fourteenth century, thus only some 400 years after Hammurabi. The inscription does indicate, however, that the Babylonians of the sixth century saw Hammurabi as a temporal point of reference that was important.

His special status led to the belief that he had been wise in every field of endeavor. A seventh-century letter from a Babylonian scholar to an unnamed Assyrian king shows how this applied to scholarly writings:

> The tablet that the king uses is defective and not in good condition. Now then, I have written to Babylon for an old tablet made by King Hammurabi and an inscription from before King Hammurabi, and I brought them.[20]

A tablet composed by Hammurabi would have been the best possible manuscript for a scholarly text. Similarly, the invention of medications was credited to him and they were considered very effective. A medical text of the first millennium includes this entry: "A salve for the eyes from Hammurabi, a proven (medication)."[21] Hammurabi became thus the example of the erudite ruler, whose skills included scholarship and medicine. Not coincidentally, those were exactly the attributes the Assyrian kings of the time tried to cultivate in their self-representations.

1,500 years after his death, Hammurabi's memory thus lived on. Soon afterwards the cuneiform tradition disappeared, however, and so did the name of Hammurabi. However, Babylonian laws had a fundamental impact on legal phraseology in the Bible and the classical world including early Rome. They followed the pattern of formulation that Hammurabi and other Mesopotamian lawgivers used, with a case by case listing of standard clauses. For example, in the Biblical book of Exodus this law appears:

If a man steals an ox or a sheep, and kills it or sells it, he shall pay five oxen for an ox, and four sheep for a sheep.[22]

The earliest Roman laws recorded exhibit the same phraseology, for example:

If someone breaks another's limb, unless he compounds for compensation with him, there shall be retaliation.[23]

Thus the Babylonian laws show parallels with the bases of the European tradition of legal thought, and may have inspired them. Yet Hammurabi's name was not attached to the laws; the Biblical, Classical, and Islamic traditions did not remember him, and he became fully forgotten.

This situation was only reversed when Europeans, in the mid-nineteenth century AD, started the archaeological exploration of the Middle East and deciphered the cuneiform scripts. By accident, Hammurabi's name appeared among the earliest inscriptions found. When in the winter of 1850 the restless English explorer, Sir Henry Austin Layard, stayed in Baghdad, he used some of the workmen he had brought with him to explore ruins. On an ancient site nearby (Tell Muhammed) they found two bronze knobs inscribed with the line, "Palace of Hammurabi." When he first published one of these in his travel account,[24] he could not read or therefore record the name, but this was soon remedied with the progress in the decipherment of cuneiform around the same time. Other sources emerged, including king lists and the Nabonidus inscription that places Hammurabi 700 years before Burnaburiash. In 1863, Joachim Ménant published a small book on the inscriptions of Hammurabi, which were still limited in number, but showed him to be a prominent king of early Babylonian history. Ménant could refer to king lists, letters, and year-names of the king, so a mixture of sources was already available 140 years ago.

The modern fame of Hammurabi was made, however, when in December 1901 and January 1902 French archaeologists at the site of Susa in western Iran excavated the law code stela in three pieces which were easily joined together. This well-preserved and detailed list of laws, phrased in the same way as Biblical laws, aroused the interest of a wide public. While some studies of Mesopotamian legal history predated the publication of the code's text in 1902, with a focus on actual documents with legal authority, the code created an avalanche of studies not seen before. Hammurabi became *the* ancient lawgiver. Legal historians wrote numerous analyses of the code itself and of its individual laws. Scholars initiated a project to translate all published contracts of Hammurabi's dynasty, under the title "Hammurabi's laws," in order to explicate the king's statements. The primary publication of contracts and legal documents from his era intensified as well.

The code's length and good state of preservation inspired scholars to see Hammurabi as the source of inspiration for all ancient Near Eastern law. The connections with Biblical law received special attention because of the obvious similarities in phraseology (and often contents) between Hammurabi's and the Bible's laws. Immediately Hammurabi was compared to Moses, the codifier of Biblical law; in 1903 two German books with the title *Moses and Hammurabi* appeared. In the early twentieth century, every educated person in Europe and the USA knew Hammurabi's name.

Hammurabi's fame as a lawgiver has survived over the decades. When in 1949 the House Chamber of the US Capitol was remodeled, it was decided to put up 23 portraits of historical figures whose work established the principles underlying American law, and Hammurabi was included. He was placed between Moses, the author of Biblical law, and Lycurgus, the traditional founder of Sparta in Greece who instituted laws, military, and political institutions. Hammurabi is probably the only king of ancient Mesopotamia whose fame is not based on his destructive powers and conquests, but on the positive benefits he brought to his people, and to humanity in general.

11

On Writing Hammurabi's Biography

Numerous biographies of famous and not-so-famous people have been written over the centuries, and continue to be published. They can be so detailed that they need to break the subject's life into segments, each period the focus of a whole book. A biography of Lyndon B. Johnson, still in progress, already consists of three volumes without even having reached his presidency.[1] It is clear that the biographer's ability to describe someone's life depends fully on access to information. A writer may face such a mass of material that selections need to be made, ignoring potentially important sources on an aspect of the subject's life that cannot be included. Today, every move of a national leader is recorded and reported, official documents proliferate in the public sphere, there are interviews, news clippings, documentaries, and a profusion of other information. For people of the past this embarrassment of riches applies less often. The paperwork and news reports produced in the time of Abraham Lincoln, for example, were much more limited than they are today. Moreover, the further back in time we reach, the more documentation has disappeared. Instead of abundance, there is often a dearth of information.

The modern biographer of a famous person from antiquity is usually faced with great gaps in the documentation. Moreover, even if ancient descriptions of someone's life exist, the historian needs to evaluate them very critically, as their purpose was usually to glorify or vilify. Just as today our biases determine how we would describe someone's accomplishments, this was also true in the past. However, unlike today, it is not always possible to find alternative evidence from the subject's time that allows a critical evaluation of the accounts.

Hammurabi of Babylon lived thirty-eight centuries ago – an enormously long time. Compared to other prominent figures of his day and for many centuries before and after him, there is much source material available, but it has grave limitations. Reading his biography is very different from reading one of Napoleon, for example. Many more aspects of his life are unknown and much that can be described is not fully certain. Some facts that we almost take for granted when reading about the life of a person in modern times is unavailable. For example, we do not know things that we would today consider the most basic information: when was Hammurabi born, how many wives and children had he, in what month and on what day did he die, and so on.

This ignorance is due to the nature of the sources on Hammurabi. The king did not write about himself, nor was there someone who knew him personally and narrated the story of his life. Even the people living much closer in time to him than we do, and who were aware of his name and fame, did not write down many anecdotes or legends about him. This may save us the eulogies and tall tales that other ancient rulers, such as Alexander of Macedon, received, but it also denies us some very basic insights into Hammurabi's life.

We also do not have a portrait of Hammurabi. On the top of the stela with his law code appears the image of a man who receives two symbols from Shamash, the god of justice. The man lifts his hand in front of his mouth in a gesture of respect. It seems very likely that the image was intended to depict the king. But does it bear any resemblance to Hammurabi? Almost exactly the same figure appears on a relief dedicated by Itur-ashdum, a servant of Hammurabi. The inscription states that Itur-ashdum dedicated the relief for the life of his king. The figure facing the inscription stands in the same pose as the man on Hammurabi's stela and is dressed the same way. Does the relief represent the king or the man who commissioned the object? Moreover, the same gesture and dress is depicted in a three-dimensional statuette of a kneeling man. That object carries the inscription:

For the god Amurru, his god, for the life of Hammurabi, king of Babylon, Lu-Nanna (broken word), the son of Sin-le'i, made for his life, a statue of a suppliant in copper and plated its face with gold. He dedicated it to him as his servant.[2]

It is very unlikely that the figurine represents King Hammurabi as the suppliant of the inscription is the commoner Lu-Nanna. Yet, he looks just like the other figures on the monuments of Hammurabi.

There is substantial evidence available on Hammurabi, however, and its opportunities and restrictions need to be understood for a proper assessment of the biographer's work. We are fully dependent on the accident of recovery for furnishing us with material. The region where Hammurabi was active – modern-day Iraq, Syria, and Iran – is covered with ancient sites, many of which have remains from his days. But few of the remains are excavated, or can be excavated. Most disappointing is the fact that Hammurabi's own capital Babylon is virtually unknown to us archaeologically. Excavators have been unable to reach the archaeological levels of this period, because high groundwater covers the remains. The possibility of excavating Hammurabi's palace seems out of the question. Only in 1907 were archaeologists able to reach levels from Hammurabi's day after a break in a dam on the Euphrates, but the exposure was very small and limited to some private houses. The extensive ruins of Babylon that are visible today date to a much later period, to the sixth century BC, and there is no reason to assume that in Hammurabi's time the city looked anything like that.

The materials we do have thus derive from subject cities within his state or from people who were not under his rule.

Plate 11.1 Statuette of a kneeling figure, excavated at Larsa. The inscription on the side states that the object was dedicated to the god Amurru for the life of King Hammurabi. The figure depicted is unlikely to be Hammurabi, but may represent the donor, Lu-Nanna (Erich Lessing/Art Resource, NY)

The most eloquent sources are letters that were written by or to Hammurabi and his courtiers, or about him by officials from other courts. As he was in the midst of most political developments in Mesopotamia in his time, other kings maintained close diplomatic contacts with him, and wanted to remain informed about his movements. The primary source in this respect is the palace archive excavated at Mari in eastern Syria on the border with modern Iraq. That city's ruler, Zimri-Lim, was at first Hammurabi's ally and later his opponent. He corresponded directly with the Babylonian king and received numerous reports about him from his envoys, generals, and some merchants. Those are the most vivid and detailed sources on Hammurabi's military actions until he defeated Zimri-Lim and took over his palace in 1761, thereby ending the stream of reports.

The Babylonian king and his government officials also corresponded extensively with regional representatives discussing administrative matters. A small, yet significant, section of this large correspondence was found in southern Babylonia, the region Hammurabi conquered in 1763. The letters are of a very different character than those from Mari since they deal with day-to-day affairs rather than the diplomatic and military struggles of the time. But, we hear the concerns of Hammurabi the man in them.

Letters provide a vivid and direct account of the questions at hand. The writers wanted to communicate information and did not bother with official rhetoric. They could report military setbacks, for example. Many of these letters were secret missives from a diplomat to his master or vice versa, and they could contain damning statements about Hammurabi one would never find in official inscriptions. However, a different problem with letters is that both the writer and the reader usually knew the context of the topic they discussed, and did not bother to describe it. We do not know these elements and can end up being confused. Moreover, unlike contracts and accounts, letters were most often not dated: thus, when an event is described, we cannot always place it in time. This creates special problems when studying the interactions of Hammurabi with one of his enemies. For example, he fought against the king of Eshnunna several years in a row, and when a letter describes a hostile encounter, we are not always able to determine its context.

The vivacity of letters can be wonderful, as they regularly quote people's words and we seem to hear them speak. We have to be cautious, however, as these were not the writings of the senders themselves – Hammurabi and his royal colleagues most likely were illiterate – but of their professional scribes. These men did not take dictation, but in consultation with their masters wrote down lists of the subjects that needed to be addressed in a missive, and then composed the letters on their own. It seems that the senders did not always take the time to have the final product read to them, and mistakes by the scribes were sometimes not caught. Despite these restrictions, the letters provide unique insights into the history of this period and the personalities of the people involved.

The city of Mari was scientifically excavated, so we know which letters belong together. One of the archive's limitations is that, after the capture of the palace, Hammurabi's officials went through it and removed the most sensitive materials – the letters to and from Hammurabi and the correspondence of Zimri-Lim with most other important rulers of the time. Those were transferred to Hammurabi's palace in Babylon (which cannot be excavated, and will probably never be found). The letters from southern Babylonia, on the other hand, were not excavated by archaeologists. They were probably dug up in the city of Larsa in the early twentieth century AD by people who sold them on the antiquities market. Today they are dispersed across several museum collections, including the Louvre in Paris, the British Museum in London, and Yale University in New Haven. Because they were illicitly excavated, scholars cannot be certain about their original whereabouts, but since the site of Larsa was pitted with holes dug in search of loot, this seems to be the likely source. The lack of secure archaeological context usually makes it impossible to determine whether or not a letter belongs to this group. When a writer addressed someone as "My Lord," we do not know whether he meant Hammurabi or some other king or higher official.

Whereas letters include straightforward reports on the issues at hand, official statements by the court about Hammurabi's achievements aimed to portray him in as positive a light as possible. Hammurabi was a great king, as were all others for whom such statements were composed; no weaknesses or mistakes would be revealed. There are various types of texts in this group of sources, some of them unique to early Babylonian history. Among the public projects that Hammurabi undertook were a number of constructions of temples and city-walls. In ancient Mesopotamia, such works were always commemorated with an inscription stating who commissioned the work and sometimes providing other information, such as that the ruler had just defeated a certain enemy. For Hammurabi such inscriptions are relatively rare, and they mention only a few events in his long and busy career.

Instead, there is a set of official statements that stretches over the duration of his entire reign – the year-names. The Babylonians distinguished years by naming them after important events in the preceding year. The first full year of a king's reign was usually called "the year that so-and-so became king," an event that had taken place some time during the previous year. For subsequent years, year-names were coined according to feats that gave special glory to the ruler. Those were often military, for example "the year that Hammurabi destroyed the wall of Mari." Non-martial deeds were usually related to the cult (the restoration of a temple, the installation of a high priest) or associated with public works (such as the excavation of a canal or the construction of a city wall). The year-names were used to date most accounts and records (though not the letters) and lists were kept to register their correct sequence. The dating system is a boon to the historian as many documents are thus securely placed in time. At the same time, the names of the years themselves give us some idea of what people at the time thought to be important events. However, since only one event every year was chosen from a multitude of royal deeds and since whatever was chosen was portrayed in a positive light, this record is very biased. A military campaign that had ended in utter failure would simply not be recorded. Still, the benefit of this system to the historian cannot be underestimated. We have the full list of all forty-three year-names of Hammurabi's reign, which provides the basic chronological structure for writing his biography.

Among the official inscriptions of Hammurabi, one stands out as the longest and the most impressive: his law code. It is carved on a conical stone stela, two and quarter meters high, with a representation in relief on the top 65 centimeters of the stone. This shows Hammurabi standing before the sun god Shamash, who is seated on a throne. That god was the protector of justice and the patron deity of the city Sippar, where the stela was originally placed. On the front and back of the stone were carved originally some 48 horizontal columns of text, only 44 of which are preserved. Hammurabi's scribes deliberately used an archaic from of script, a sign that the authors wanted to give great weight to the contents by making it look old. The text includes a long prologue honoring Hammurabi's achievements as a protector of the cities of his country, between 275 and 300 laws, and an epilogue celebrating the fact that he granted justice. The stone stela was carved after Hammurabi's thirty-eighth year of rule, and it was only one of several such monuments and clay tablets that contained part of his laws. Some of those were written earlier in his reign. He seems to have erected the stone stelae in public places in several cities, in order to broadcast his adherence to justice. The best preserved example was still standing in Sippar 600 years after Hammurabi's death, when a king of Elam, Shutruk-Nahhunte I, raided Babylonia and took it back home with him. That is why the stela was excavated at Susa by French archaeologists in 1901–2, and ended up in the Louvre museum.

Some courtiers of his reign also composed hymns in honor of Hammurabi, probably on the occasion of special events, such as festivals. Only a small number of those are known, and almost all of them exist in a very fragmentary state. They praise his connections to various gods and his success in warfare.

Any well-functioning state requires some type of administration and Hammurabi's was no exception. During his reign the government bureaucracy recorded agricultural activity, trade, palace expenditures, and the like, while private citizens kept records as evidence of the legality of sales and so on. Those were written in substantial numbers in Hammurabi's time, a typical feature of early Babylonian bureaucracy. Wherever excavations take place in the area of Hammurabi's kingdom, such records are regularly found. While they most often do not document that king's actions, they do illustrate general administrative practices in his reign and shed light on the economic situation at the time. This mundane source allows us to round out the person of Hammurabi to some extent, as it reveals the living conditions in his state.

The clay tablets on which the letters, accounts, and documents of Mesopotamia were impressed survived for millennia in the climate of Iraq. Left behind in the soil in the ruins of buildings, those objects did not disintegrate. The historian is thus blessed with a relative abundance of written documentation that is absent for many ancient cultures. A tablet is a fragile object, however, and damage to it is easily done. This explains why so many texts have breaks in them. Parts of the surface are erased or whole pieces broken off. The scholar must try to restore the gaps through parallels with similar texts, or by searching for meaning in the faint traces. The frustration can be great. It is most irritating when a crucial passage is partly illegible, and this often is the case. Several suggestions can be made that lead to very different historical reconstructions. The following example shows how maddening this can be. There exists a letter written to an administrator in Larsa by Hammurabi's son and successor, Samsuiluna, just upon his accession to the throne. It starts out with these sentences:

To Etel-pi-Marduk say, thus speaks Samsuiluna: The king my father . . . I have taken [my place] on the throne of [my father's house] in order to [rule] the land.[3]

Only the first cuneiform sign is preserved of the last part of the statement about Hammurabi, indicated as . . . in the translation. The simplest restoration would be to translate the broken passage as "is ill," and several scholars have suggested this. If correct, it reveals that Hammurabi was ill late in life, and was already succeeded on the throne by his son before he died. Many scholars cannot accept that reconstruction, however, because they believe that a major king like Hammurabi would not have given up the throne before his death. They translate instead that Hammurabi "was ill," or "became ill and died," which would support their presupposition about the succession of kings. The historical supposition becomes thus the basis of the reconstruction of a source, rather than the other way around. In the end, no amount of discussion will ever solve this problem (unless another copy of the letter is found). An unusual tidbit of information about Hammurabi that was so tantalizingly close has been lost.

A biography of Hammurabi is thus written on the basis of many fewer sources than exist for many other personalities in world history. Many aspects of his life are vague or totally unknown to us. Besides being a warrior and ruler, he was a husband and father, a man who must have had friends and enemies, who must have had his moments of pride and fear. These are attributes that are almost impossible to uncover, as our sources are mostly silent on them. The lack of information denies us an understanding of Hammurabi as a human being. How can we interpret his actions on a psychological level, if we do not really know anything about his relationships with others? For a subject living today or in the recent past we would find such information indispensable in a biography.

Similarly, we cannot always understand Hammurabi's achievements, since we do not know the context in which they took place. There is insufficient information on other kings who lived in his time to judge, for example, how exceptional Hammurabi's conquests were. If his neighbors were spent forces, it was not such a big deal that he defeated them. The background for his actions is too vague for us to comprehend their reasons. We can describe them, but we cannot contextualize them.

On the one hand, the material on Hammurabi is so fragmentary that it leaves much of his life in the dark; on the other hand it exceeds what we know about others of his time by far. The distance in time and circumstances hides much about Hammurabi that we would like to know, and the result of our research is a fragmentary picture of this man. We can clearly establish, however, that his accomplishments were great and that his name rightly deserves to be remembered.

Glossary

Abi-eshuh: the second successor of Hammurabi as king of Babylon, who ruled from 1711 to 1684.

Adad: the Babylonian storm god. In Amorite his name is Addu.

Akkadian: the general term used to indicate the Semitic language of Mesopotamia. It had various dialects, including Babylonian in the south and Assyrian in the north. People speaking and writing the language are called Akkadians.

Ammisaduqa: the fourth successor of Hammurabi as king of Babylon, who ruled from 1648 to 1628.

Amorite: a west Semitic language spoken by many inhabitants of Mesopotamia and Syria in the early centuries of the second millennium BC. The language differs from Akkadian in grammar and vocabulary. No complete text was ever written down in Amorite, and we mostly know the language because some people's recorded names were Amorite. A person speaking Amorite is also called an Amorite.

Anatolia: the name used to refer to the area of Turkey in antiquity.

Assur: a city on the Tigris with an important religious role. In later centuries it became the political center of the region.

Atamrum: the ruler of a small north Mesopotamian state who became Elam's viceroy in the region, but later switched sides to Mari.

Babylon: the capital city of Hammurabi's kingdom and seat of his dynasty, located south of Baghdad in modern Iraq. After Hammurabi it remained the political center of the region for another 1500 years. The term is also used here to refer to Hammurabi's kingdom as a whole.

Babylonia: the region of southern Mesopotamia, that is from the modern city of Baghdad to the Persian Gulf. The term is used here as a geographical designation only, not as a political one.

Babylonian: the Akkadian dialect used in Babylonia.

Benjaminite: tribesmen in the region to the north of Mari.

city-state: the political organization that integrates a city and its immediate surroundings into one small-scale state.

cuneiform: the modern name for the script used in the Middle East throughout most of its ancient history. The signs were impressed in clay or carved on stone, and its lines resembled wedges. The script was not alphabetic, but each sign rendered a full word or a syllable.

Dilmun: the name of an island state in the Persian Gulf, modern Bahrain.

Ekallatum: the capital city of Ishme-Dagan located on the Tigris river.

Elam: a state in south-western Iran that controlled the southern lowlands east of the Tigris river and the highlands of modern-day Fars.

Eshnunna: the state located in the Diyala river valley to the east of the Tigris, and the name of its capital (modern Tell Asmar).

Gutians: people from the Zagros mountains, ruled by a queen, who were often allied with Hammurabi's enemies east of the Tigris.

Habur: a river in northern Syria that drains into the Euphrates.

Hit: a border city on the Euphrates between the kingdoms of Mari and Babylon.

homer: the unit of capacity to measure dry goods, such as grain. The amount corresponds to what one donkey can carry.

Ibal-pi-El: an important Mari general and author of many letters to Zimri-Lim.

Ibal-pi-El II: king of Eshnunna in the early part of Hammurabi's reign. He ruled from 1779 to 1765, and was overthrown by a coalition of Elam, Babylon, and Mari.

Inanna: a southern Babylonian goddess.

Ishme-Dagan: the son of Shamshi-Adad who ruled the Tigris area around Ekallatum and Assur. He maintained erratic diplomatic relations with Hammurabi.

Isin: a central Babylonian city.

Khanean: the name of Bedouin tribesmen around Mari.

Kingdom of Upper Mesopotamia: the state created by King Shamshi-Adad, which at its height controlled the entire northern zone of Mesopotamia from the Zagros Mountains to the Euphrates river in northern Syria.

Kudur-Mabuk: the father of kings Warad-Sin and Rim-Sin of Larsa.

Kudu-zulush: the *sukkal* of Susa who governed Eshnunna.

Larsa: an important city in the south of Babylonia, which had been the seat of a leading royal house for two centuries before Hammurabi's conquest. Hammurabi used it as the administrative center of the southern province.

Malgium: a state located on the Tigris, east of Babylon.

Marduk: the patron deity of the city Babylon.

Mari: a city located on the middle Euphrates river, in the east of modern Syria, which controlled traffic between Mesopotamia and

Syria. Its palace archive of cuneiform tablets provides the richest source of information on the history of the period.

Mashkan-shapir: the second capital of the state of Larsa, located in the north-east of the state.

Mutiabal: the region around the city Kazallu, just to the north of Babylon, subject to Hammurabi.

Mutu-numaha: the younger son of Hammurabi.

Nippur: a central Babylonian city with special religious importance as the home of the god Enlil, head of the Sumerian pantheon.

Qatna: a state in the south-west of Syria, whose support was sought by Mesopotamian rulers in their internecine disputes.

Qattara: a small city in northern Mesopotamia. Excavations there recovered a rich archive of letters and documents of a vassal of Hammurabi.

Rim-Sin: a king of Larsa who ruled from 1822 to 1763, when Hammurabi dethroned him.

river ordeal: a judicial procedure whereby the river god is asked to judge the validity of a claim. The accused or a representative is thrown into the water and has to complete a difficult task. Failure to complete it indicates guilt.

Samsuiluna: the son and first successor of Hammurabi, who ruled Babylon from 1749 to 1712.

Shamash: the Babylonian sun god and god of justice. He was the patron deity of the city Sippar.

Shamash-hazir: Hammurabi's official in the south responsible for the supervision of field assignments.

Shamshi-Adad: the creator of the kingdom of Upper Mesopotamia who dominated Mesopotamia at the time of Hammurabi's accession to the throne. He ruled from around 1808 to 1776.

shekel: a Babylonian weight measuring about 8 grams.

Shutruk-Nahhunte I: the Elamite king who raided Babylonia and took the stela of Hammurabi to Susa in the twelfth century.

Silli-Sin: the ephemeral king of Eshnunna after Elam's withdrawal. Married to Hammurabi's daughter.

Sim'alites: members of one of the Amorite tribes in northern Syria, among whom Zimri-Lim of Mari belonged.

Sin-bel-aplim: Hammurabi's minister of foreign affairs.

Sin-iddinam: Hammurabi's highest representative in the southern province of Yamutbal, stationed in Larsa.

Sin-muballit: a) Hammurabi's father. He ruled Babylon from 1812 to 1793.
b) brother of Rim-Sin of Larsa who governed Mashkan-shapir.

Sippar: an important city of the state of Babylon, located to the north of the capital. It housed a royal palace where Hammurabi regularly stayed.

Siwe-palar-huppak: the *sukkalmah* of Elam who conquered Eshnunna. In Babylonian sources he is regularly called Sheplarpak.

Subartu: the name the Babylonians gave to regions in the north. It does not refer to a specific state but to the area in general.

Suhu: the area along the Euphrates to the north-west of Babylonia.

sukkal: the title of the Elamite ruler of Susa. The Babylonian texts that refer to him use this term in preference to the ruler's name.

sukkalmah: the title of the ruler of the entire kingdom of Elam.

Sumerian: the non-Semitic language that was originally spoken in the south of Babylonia. It had probably died out as a spoken language in the beginning of the second millennium, but continued to be written in legal and administrative documents, as well as in royal inscriptions and literature.

Sumuditana: the oldest son of Hammurabi.

Susa: the capital city of the state of Elam.

Suteans: members of one of the Amorite tribes in Mesopotamia.

Turukkum: highland people from the Zagros mountains to the north-east of Assur.

Uruk: a southern Babylonian city.

Warad-Sin: the brother and predecessor of King Rim-Sin of Larsa.

Yahdun-Lim: the king of Mari before its conquest by Shamshi-Adad. He ruled until around 1798.

Yamkhad: an important kingdom in north-western Syria around the city of Aleppo. Its king was a desirable ally to the powers in Mesopotamia and the father-in-law of king Zimri-Lim of Mari.

Yamutbal: the name of the southern state whose capital was Larsa. Under Hammurabi the name was used to refer to the province of the south.

Yarim-Addu: one of Hammurabi's representatives in Babylon.

Yashmah-Addu: the younger son of Shamshi-Adad who ruled Mari during his father's lifetime, but disappeared when Zimri-Lim conquered the city.

year-name: the name Babylonians used to identify a particular year. The name was based on important events in the preceding year. A list of the names enabled scribes to keep a chronological order of records.

Zagros Mountains: the mountain range that forms the border between modern-day Iraq and Iran. In antiquity it was home to a number of peoples, usually with hostile relations to the states in the low-lands of Mesopotamia.

Zimri-Addu: an important Mari general and author of many letters.

Zimri-Lim: king of Mari during most of Hammurabi's reign. He was an important ally of Babylon, but was overthrown in 1761 when the relations soured.

Notes

Chapter 1

1 ARM I no. 108 = Durand 1997 no. 34.
2 ARM IV no. 26 = Durand 1998 no. 534.
3 Durand 1997 no. 318 and Durand 2000 no. 1027.
4 Van Koppen 1997, 420 lines 2'–14'.
5 ARM V no. 14 = Durand 2000 no. 916.
6 ARM IV no. 81 = Durand 1998 no. 539.
7 Grayson 1987, 63–5. The name of the king is not preserved, but the arguments that the inscription was commissioned by Shamshi-Adad are strong.
8 Dossin 1938, 117–18.
9 Finkelstein 1969, 528 § 20.
10 Finkelstein 1969, 527 § 8.
11 Frayne 1990, 354.
12 CH ii 23–31 = Roth 1997, 77.
13 CH iii 18–23 = Roth 1997, 78.
14 Frayne 1990, 335.

Chapter 2

1 Babylonian sources often refer to him as Sheplarpak.
2 ARM XXV no. 5 quoted from Durand 1986, 119 n. 26.
3 For example, Shaduppum (= modern Tell Harmal).
4 A.3618, quoted from Charpin 1999, 122.
5 A.3618, quoted from Charpin and Durand 1991, 63.
6 ARM XXVI/2 no. 362 lines 5–10.

7   ARM XXVI/2 no. 362 lines 12–14.
8   ARM XXVI/2 no. 362 lines 25–37.
9   ARM XXVI/2 no. 362 lines 38–51.
10 See Joannès in ARM 26/2, 242–51.
11 ARM XIV no. 104+, quoted from Charpin 1993, 199–200, also Durand 1998 no. 548.
12 ARM XIV no. 103 lines 8–9.
13 ARM XXVI/2 no. 303 lines 47'–9'.
14 Charpin 1999, 124.
15 Charpin 1990, 111–12 lines 12–17.
16 ARM II no. 48 lines 5–24 = Durand 1998 no. 559.
17 ARM II no. 118 lines 4–23 = Durand 1998 no. 577.
18 Durand 1998 no. 579.
19 ARM XXV no. 815 rev, 3'–18', quoted from Joannès 1989, 147.
20 ARM XXVII no. 12 rev 1'–5' = Durand 1998 no. 567.
21 ARM XIV no. 76 lines 18–28 = Durand 1997 no. 260.
22 ARM XXVI/2 no. 363.
23 ARM XXVI/2 no. 369 rev 15'–20'.
24 ARM XXVII no. 140 lines 15–21.
25 ARM XXVII no. 142 lines 6–10.
26 ARM XXVII no. 141 lines 24–46.
27 A.2996 quoted from Charpin 1999, 125.
28 ARM XXVII no. 146 lines 21–30.
29 A.1931 quoted from Charpin 1999, 126.
30 ARM XXVII no. 149 lines 3–22.
31 ARM XXVI/2 no. 383 lines 8'–12'.

Chapter 3

1   ARM XXVI/2 no. 367.
2   ARM XXVI/2 no. 367.
3   ARM XXVI/2 no. 372 lines 27–40.
4   ARM XXVI/2 no. 385 lines 1'–21'.
5   ARM XXVI/2 no. 385 lines 34'–44'.
6   ARM XXVI/2 no. 383 lines 3–12.
7   ARM XXVII no. 156 lines 4–10.
8   ARM XXVII no. 156 lines 1'–7'.
9   ARM XXVII no. 161 lines 33–52.
10 M.13832 lines 7'–10', quoted from Charpin 1999, 127.
11 ARM II no. 24+ = Durand 1998 no. 586.

Chapter 4

1   ARM II no. 49 = Durand 1997 no. 309.
2   Charpin 1991, 149 i 1 13 = Durand 1997 no. 281.
3   Charpin 1991, 149 iii 28–37 = Durand 1997 no. 281.
4   Charpin 1991, 149 iv 19′–23′ = Durand 1997 no. 281.
5   Charpin 1991, 161 lines 7–20 = Durand 1997 no. 282.
6   ARM XXVI/1 no. 25.
7   ARM XIII no. 34 = Durand 1998 no. 696.
8   Kupper 1990, 338 lines 60–4.
9   A 3354+, quoted from Charpin 1991, 163.
10 Dossin 1972, 57–8 = Durand 1997 no. 300.
11 ARM XXVI/2 no. 373 lines 9–17.
12 Frayne 1990, 583 and 588.
13 Frayne 1990, 587.
14 ARM XXVI/2 no. 370 lines 38′–42′.
15 ARM XXVI/2 no. 372 lines 3–26. The words enclosed by square
    brackets [ ] are suggested restorations of breaks in the tablet.
16 ARM XXVI/2 no. 373 lines 43–6.
17 ARM XXVI/2 no. 373 lines 3–27.
18 Ozan 1997, 295–8 no. 142.
19 ARM XXV no. 19.
20 Bonechi 1993.
21 ARM VI no. 27 = Durand 1997 no. 424.
22 Richardson forthcoming.
23 Frayne 1990, 355–6.

Chapter 5

1   ARM XXVI/2 no. 384 lines 19′–22′.
2   ARM XXVI/2 no. 371.
3   ARM XXVI/1 no. 104 quoted from Charpin 1999, 118.
4   ARM XXVI/1 no. 104 quoted from Charpin 1999, 118.
5   Charpin ARM XXVI/2, 154 n. 93.
6   ARM XXVI/2 no. 370 lines 48′–53′.
7   ARM XXVI/2 no. 384.
8   ARM XXVI/2 no. 526 lines 6–23.
9   Dalley 1976 no. 135.
10 Dalley 1976 no. 70.
11 Dalley 1976 no. 68.

Chapter 6

1   ARM II no. 87 = Durand 1997 no. 163.
2   ARM XXVI/1 no. 249 lines 3–30.
3   ARM XXVI/1 no. 40 lines 3–8.
4   ARM XXVI/2 no. 449 lines 3–67.
5   ARM XXVI/2 no. 468 lines 3–21.
6   ARM XXVI/2 no. 468 lines 6′–26′.
7   ARM XXVI/1 no. 160 lines 1′–6′.
8   ARM II no. 21 = Durand 1997 no. 350.
9   ARM II no. 21 = Durand 1997 no. 350.
10 ARM XXVI/2 no. 381 lines 6′–26′.
11 ARM II no. 24+ = Durand 1998 no. 586.
12 Durand 1997 no. 289. Charpin and Ziegler 2003, 234 consider the accusation of betrayal to refer to Ishme-Dagan of Ekallatum.
13 ARM XXVI/1 no. 185–*bis* = Durand 2000 no. 1145.
14 ARM XXVI/1 no. 212 lines 1′–9′ = Durand 2000 no. 1146.
15 ARM XXVI/1 no. 209 lines 8–13 = Durand 2000 no. 939.
16 ARM XXVI/1 no. 131 lines 4–21. Square brackets [ ] indicate a damaged part of the tablet.
17 Ziegler 2002, 252–4 no. 25.
18 Sasson 1998, 466–7.
19 Charpin 1995, 31 no. 2.
20 Charpin and Ziegler 2003, 245 n. 714 refer to the statement by Mari's earliest excavator, André Parrot, that four lists with names of Babylonian soldiers were found. The one that was supposedly dated with the name of Hammurabi's 32nd year can no longer be located. On pp. 250–2, they also publish a legal record that refers to a claim "during the reign of Zimri-Lim," which they interpret as an indication that the record is dated later than his reign.
21 Frayne 1990, 345 lines 27–30.
22 AbB 2, 88 line 20′.
23 CH ii 37–47 = Roth 1997, 77–8.
24 CH iv 32–44 = Roth 1997, 80.

Chapter 7

1   Frayne 1990, 341 lines 28–37.
2   Frayne 1990, 341 lines 17–20.

3 Lion 1994, 223 no. 120.
4 AbB 13 no. 48 lines 1–9.
5 AbB 4 no. 54.
6 AbB 4 no. 115.
7 Birot 1969 no. 1.
8 AbB 4 no. 31.
9 E.g., AbB 9 no. 190.
10 AbB 4 no. 79.
11 AbB 4 no. 22.
12 AbB 2 no. 27.
13 AbB 2 no. 55.
14 AbB 4 no. 39.
15 AbB 4 no. 85.
16 AbB 9 no. 78.
17 AbB 2 no. 33.
18 AbB 13 no. 11.
19 AbB 2 nos. 8, 36, 39; AbB 4 no. 140.
20 AbB 2 no. 39.
21 AbB 2 no. 57.
22 AbB 2 no. 11.
23 AbB 13 no. 41.
24 AbB 13 no. 18.
25 AbB 13 no. 21.
26 Bonechi 1993.
27 AbB 13 no. 25.
28 AbB 13 no. 10.
29 AbB 4 no. 16.
30 Szlechter 1953, 97; Landsberger 1955, 126.
31 CH § 26 = Roth 1997, 85–6.
32 AbB 9 no. 32.

Chapter 8

1 CH iii 55–64 = Roth 1997, 79. CH xlvii 1–8 = Roth 1997, 133.
2 CH li 40–9 = Roth 1997, 139.
3 CH xlvii 1–8 = Roth 1997, 133.
4 CH § 42 = Roth 1997, 89.
5 CH § 45 = Roth 1997, 89.
6 CH § 53 = Roth 1997, 91.
7 CH § 54 = Roth 1997, 91–2.

8   Roth 1997, 75.
9   Compare Saggs 1988, 184–7.
10 CH §§ 196–7 = Roth 1997, 121.
11 CH §§ 229–30 = Roth 1997, 125.
12 CH §§ 198–9 = Roth 1997, 121.
13 CH § 202 = Roth 1997, 121.
14 CH § 123 = Roth 1977, 104.
15 Roth 1997, 6.
16 AbB 10 no. 6.
17 CH § 178 = Roth 1997, 117.
18 CH § 54 = Roth 1997, 67.
19 CH § 251 = Roth 1997, 128.
20 AbB 9 no. 197.
21 CH xlviii 3–38 = Roth 134–5.
22 CH xlviii 59–94 = Roth 1997, 135.

Chapter 9

1   Thureau-Dangin 1936 = Durand 2000 no. 1271.
2   ARM II no. 23 = Durand 1998 no. 590.
3   ARM XXVI/1 no. 102, after Pongratz-Leisten 1999, 146–7.
4   ARM XXVI/1 no. 160.
5   ARM XXVI/2 no. 385.
6   ARM XXVI/2 no. 471 lines 8'–12', see also ARM XXVI/2 no. 381.
7   ARM II no. 76 = Durand 1997 no. 404.
8   Durand 1992, 47–9 quoted after Durand 1997 no. 289 and Sasson 2001, 330.
9   ARM XXVI/2 no. 365 = Durand 1998 no. 580.
10 ARM XXVI/2 no. 365–bis.
11 ARM XXVI/2 no. 384 line 44', see chapter 5.

Chapter 10

1   CH xlvii 22–31 = Roth 1997, 133.
2   CH xlvii 32, 43 = Roth 1997, 133.
3   King 1898 no. 60 col VII–VIII.
4   Gadd and Legrain 1928 no. 146.
5   Gadd and Legrain 1928 no. 146.
6   Sjöberg 1961, 51–2.

7 Sjöberg 1961, 52.
8 Gadd and Legrain 1928 no. 146 col. V–VI.
9 Çig, Kizilyay, and Kramer 1969, 111 Ni 4225.
10 Groneberg 1997, 87.
11 Çig, Kizilyay, and Kramer 1969, 112 Ni 4577 rev II 4.
12 Held 1961, 9.
13 Roth 1997, 75.
14 Sjöberg 1991.
15 Lambert 1989.
16 Frame 1995, 291, 295, and 319.
17 Frame 1995, 304 and 316.
18 Frame 1995, 318.
19 Langdon 1912, 238.
20 Parpola 1993 no. 155.
21 Oppenheim 1977, 366 n. 25.
22 *Exodus* chapter 22, 1–2 (RSV).
23 After Coleman-Norton 1952, 18.
24 Layard 1853, 477.

Chapter 11

1 Robert R. Caro, *The Years of Lyndon Johnson*, New York: Alfred Knopf, vols. 1–3, 1982–2002.
2 Frayne 1990, 360.
3 Dossin 1933 no. 76. The words enclosed by square brackets [ ] are suggested restorations of breaks in the tablet.

Bibliography

Birot, M. 1969. *Tablettes économiques et administratives d'époque babylonienne ancienne.* Paris: Librairie orientaliste Paul Geuthner.

Bonechi, M. 1993. "Conscription à Larsa après la conquête babylonienne." *MARI* 7: 129–64.

Charpin, D. 1990. "Une alliance contre l'Elam et le rituel du *lipit napištim.*" In *Mélanges Jean Perrot.* Edited by F. Vallat. Paris: Éditions Recherche sur les Civilisations: 109–18.

Charpin, D. 1991. "Un traité entre Zimri-Lim de Mari et Ibâl-pî-El II d'Ešnunna." In *Marchands, diplomates et empereurs. Etudes sur la civilisation mésopotamienne offertes à Paul Garelli.* Edited by D. Charpin and F. Joannès. Paris: Éditions Recherche sur les Civilisations: 139–66.

Charpin, D. 1993. "Données nouvelles sur la poliorcétique à l'époque paléo-babylonienne." *MARI* 7: 193–203.

Charpin, D. 1995. "La fin des archives dans le palais de Mari." *Revue d'Assyriologie* 89: 29–40.

Charpin, D. 1999. "Hammu-rabi de Babylone et Mari: nouvelles sources, nouvelles perspectives." In *Babylon. Focus mesopotamischer Geschichte, Wiege früher Gelehrsamkeit, Mythos in der Moderne.* Edited by J. Renger. Saarbrücken: SDV Saarbrücker Druckerei und Verlag: 111–30.

Charpin, D. and Durand, J.-M. 1991. "La suzeraineté de l'empereur (sukkalmah) d'Elam sur la Mésopotamie et le 'nationalisme' amorrite." In *Mésopotamie et Elam.* Edited by L. de Meyer. Ghent: University of Ghent: 59–66.

Charpin, D. and Ziegler, N. 2003. *Florilegium marianum V. Mari et le Proche-Orient à l'époque amorrite. Essai d'histoire politique.* Paris: SEPOA.

Çig, M., Kizilyay, H., and Kramer, S. N. 1969. *Istanbul Arkeoloji Müzelerinde Bulunan. Sumer Edebî Tablet ve Parçalari* -I. Ankara: Türk Tarih Kurumu Basimevi.

Coleman-Norton, P. R. 1952. *The Twelve Tables.* Princeton: Department of Classics.

Dalley, S. 1976. *The Old Babylonian Tablets from Tell al Rimah.* British School of Archaeology in Iraq.

Dossin, G. 1933. *Lettres de la première dynastie babylonienne* (*Textes cunéiformes* XVII). Paris: Librarie orientaliste Paul Geuthner.

Dossin, G. 1938. "Les archives épistolaires du palais de Mari." *Syria* 19: 105–26.

Dossin, G. 1972. "Le *madārum* dans les «archives royales de Mari»." In *Gesellschaftsklassen im Alten Zweistromland.* Edited by D. O. Edzard. Munich: Bayerische Akademie der Wissenschaften: 53–63.

Durand, J.-M. 1986. "Fragment rejoints pour une histoire Elamite." In *Fragmenta historiae Elamicae. Mélanges offerts à M. J. Steve.* Edited by L. de Meyer, H. Gasche, F. Vallat. Paris: Éditions Recherche sur les Civilisations: 111–28.

Durand, J.-M. 1992. "Espionnage et guerre froide: la fin de Mari." In *Florilegium marianum. Recueil d'études en l'honneur de Michel Fleury.* Edited by J.-M. Durand. Paris: SEPOA: 39–52.

Durand, J.-M. 1997. *Les documents épistolaires de Mari* I. Paris: Éditions du Cerf.

Durand, J.-M. 1998. *Les documents épistolaires de Mari* II. Paris: Éditions du Cerf.

Durand, J.-M. 2000. *Les documents épistolaires de Mari* III. Paris: Éditions du Cerf.

Finkelstein, J. J. 1969. "The Edict of Ammisaduqa." In *Ancient Near Eastern Texts Relating to the Old Testament.* Edited by J. B. Pritchard. Third edition. Princeton: Princeton University Press: 526–8.

Frame, G. 1995. *Rulers of Babylonia. From the Second Dynasty of Isin to the End of the Assyrian Domination* (1157–612 BC Toronto: The University of Toronto Press.

Frayne, D. 1990. *Old Babylonian Period* (2003–1595 BC Toronto: The University of Toronto Press.

Gadd, C. J. and Legrain, L. 1928. *Ur Excavations Texts I. Royal Inscriptions.* London and Philadelphia: British Museum and the University Museum of the University of Pennsylvania.

Grayson, A. K. 1987. *Assyrian Rulers of the Third and Second Millennia BC to 1115 BC Toronto: The University of Toronto Press.

Groneberg, B. 1997. *Lob der Ištar. Gebet und Ritual an die altbabylonische Venusgöttin.* Groningen: Styx.

Held, M. 1961. "A faithful lover in an Old Babylonian Dialogue." *Journal of Cuneiform Studies* 15: 1–26.

Joannès, F. 1989. "La culture matérielle à Mari (IV): Les méthodes de pesée." *Revue d'Assyriologie* 83: 113–52.

King, L. 1898. *The Letters and Inscriptions of Hammurabi, King of Babylon, about B2200* vol. I. London: Luzac and Co.

Kupper, J.-R. 1990. "Une lettre du général Yassi-Dagan." *MARI* 6: 337–47.

Lambert, W. G. 1989. "The Laws of Hammurabi in the First Millennium." In *Reflets des deux fleuves. Volume de mélanges offerts à André Finet.* Edited by M. Lebeau and P. Talon. Louvain: Peeters: 95–8.

Landsberger, B. 1955. "Remarks on the Archive of the Soldier Ubarum." *Journal of Cuneiform Studies* 9: 121–131.

Langdon, S. 1912. *Die neubabylonischen Königsinschriften.* Leipzig: Hinrichs'sche Buchhandlung.

Layard, A. H. 1853. *Discoveries in the Ruins of Nineveh and Babylon.* London: John Murray.

Lion, B. 1994. "Des princes de Babylone à Mari." In *Florilegium marianum* II. *Recueil d'études à la mémoire de Maurice Birot.* Edited by D. Charpin and J.-M. Durand. Paris: SEPOA: 221–34.

Ménant, J. 1863. *Inscriptions de Hammourabi, Roi de Babylone (xvième siècle avant J.-C.).* Paris: Librarie Orientale Benjamin Duprat.

Oppenheim, A. L. 1977. *Ancient Mesopotamia. Portrait of a Dead Civilization.* Second edition. Chicago and London: University of Chicago Press.

Ozan, G. 1997. "Les lettres de Manatân." In *Florilegium marianum* III. *Recueil d'études à la mémoire de Marie-Thérèse Barrelet.* Edited by D. Charpin and J.-M. Durand. Paris: SEPOA: 291–305.

Parpola, S. 1993. *Letters from Assyrian and Babylonian Scholars.* Helsinki: Helsinki University Press.

Pongratz-Leisten, B. 1999. *Herrschaftswissen in Mesopotamien. Formen der Kommunikation zwischen Gott und König im 2. und 1. Jahrtausend v. Chr.* Helsinki: Helsinki University Press.

Richardson, S. Forthcoming. "Axes Against Ešnunna." *Orientalia.*

Roth, M. T. 1997. *Law Collections from Mesopotamia and Asia Minor.* Second edition. Atlanta: Scholars Press.

Saggs, H. W. F. 1988. *The Greatness that was Babylon*. London: Sidgwick & Jackson.

Sasson, J. M. 1998. "The King and I. A Mari King in Changing Perceptions." *Journal of the American Oriental Society* 118: 543–70.

Sasson, J. M. 2001. "On Reading the Diplomatic Letters in the Mari Archives." In *Amurru* 2. *Mari, Ébla et les Hourrites. Dix ans de travaux*. Edited by D. Charpin and J.-M. Durand. Paris: Éditions Recherche sur les Civilisations: 329–38.

Sjöberg, Å. 1961. "Ein Selbstpreis des Königs Hammurabi von Babylon." *Zeitschrift für Assyriologie* 54: 51–70.

Sjöberg, Å. 1991. "Was there a Sumerian Version of the Laws of Hammurabi?" In *Velles Paraules. Ancient Near Eastern Studies in Honor of Miguel Civil. Aula Orientalis 9*. Edited by P. Michalowski et al. Barcelona: 219–25.

Szlechter, E. 1953. "Les tablettes juridiques datées du règne d'Abî-ešuḫ conservées au Musée d'art et d'histoire de Genève." *Journal of Cuneiform Studies* 7: 81–99.

Thureau-Dangin, F. 1936. "Textes de Mâri." *Revue d'Assyriologie* 33: 169–79.

Van Koppen, F. 1997. "L'expédition à Tilmun et la révolte des bédouins." *MARI* 8: 417–29.

Ziegler, N. 2002. "Le royaume d'Ekallâtum et son horizon géographique." In *Florilegium marianum VI. Recueil d'études à la mémoire d'André Parrot*. Edited by D. Charpin and J.-M. Durand. Paris: SEPOA: 211–74.

Guide to Further Reading

Most studies of Hammurabi's reign were published before a large number of important Mari letters were known, and are thus out of date. An excellent short description in English is Jack M. Sasson, "King Hammurabi of Babylon," in *Civilizations of the Ancient Near East* (J. M. Sasson, ed.), New York: Charles Scribner's Sons, 1995: vol. II, 901–915. Very recently a French survey of Hammurabi's reign with a discussion of Babylonian society was published by a leading member of the team that is in charge of the Mari material: Dominique Charpin, *Hammu-rabi de Babylone*, Paris: Presses Universitaires de France, 2003 (the book appeared after the manuscript of this biography was completed). A somewhat older German book discusses the history of Hammurabi's dynasty and many aspects of the culture, society, and economy of the time: Horst Klengel, *König Hammurapi und der Alltag Babylons*, Düsseldorf/Zürich: Artemis & Winkler, 1999.

Hammurabi's royal inscriptions are edited and translated into English by Douglas Frayne, *Old Babylonian Period (2003–1595 BC)*, Toronto: The University of Toronto Press, 1990. His correspondence with Babylonian officials is translated into English and German in the series *Altbabylonische Briefe in Umschrift und Übersetzung*, Leiden: E. J. Brill. The Mari letters are mostly published in the French series *Archives royales de Mari* issued by various publishers in Paris. The year-names of Hammurabi's dynasty are collected and studied in Malcolm J. A. Horsnell, *The Year-Names of the First Dynasty of Babylon*, 2 vols., Hamilton: McMaster University Press, 1999. For Sumerian literary hymns in honor of Hammurabi, see the website of *The Electronic Text Corpus of Sumerian Literature*, The Oriental

Institute, The University of Oxford, http://www-etcsl.ox.ac.uk. Another example in Sumerian and Akkadian and carved on stone, was re-edited by N. Wasserman, "CT 21, 40–42 – A Bilingual Report of an Oracle with a Royal Hymn of Hammurabi," *Revue d'Assyriologie* 86 (1992), 1–18.

A general book on the entire history and culture of Babylonia is H. W. F. Saggs, *The Greatness that was Babylon*, London: Sidgwick & Jackson, 1988. Numerous detailed studies on Hammurabi's code and its legal implications have appeared; for a survey see Samuel Greengus, "Legal and Social Institutions of Ancient Mesopotamia," in *Civilizations of the Ancient Near East* (J. M. Sasson, ed.), New York: Charles Scribner's Sons, 1995: vol. I, 469–84, and its bibliography. The function of the code continues to be debated. The discussion was started by J. Bottéro, "Le «code» de Hammurabi," *Annali della Scuola normale superiore di Pisa, Classe di Lettere e Filosofia*, III/xii: 4 (1982) 409–44, translated into English in J. Bottéro, *Mesopotamia: writing, reasoning, and the gods*, Chicago: The University of Chicago Press, 1992, 156–84. Some recent English articles are M. T. Roth, "The Law Collection of King Hammurabi: Toward an Understanding of Codification and Text," and R. Westbrook, "Codification and Canonization," both in *La codification des lois dans l'antiquité* (Ed. Lévy, ed.), Paris: de Boccard, 2000, 9–47.

For a general introduction to the history of the ancient Near East, see Marc Van De Mieroop, *A History of the Ancient Near East, ca. 3000–323 BC*, Oxford: Blackwell Publishing, 2004. Numerous maps and illustrations can be found in Michael Roaf, *Cultural Atlas of Mesopotamia and the Ancient Near East*, New York: Facts on File, 1990.

Index

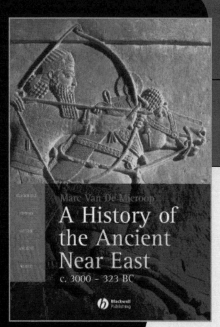

Printed and bound in the UK by
CPI Antony Rowe, Eastbourne